D1478282

Continued Praise for ...*the Best Policy*

"This book speaks to the importance of providing for families and their needs through the effective use of Life Insurance Trusts. Tate's book makes a very complicated subject understandable, and he provides real-life examples of how his management of irrevocable life insurance trusts has made a difference in the lives of families who have benefited from his trusted services. The Groome family has been providing critical life insurance solutions to our family and our business for three generations. Their comprehensive life insurance planning and management has proven to be invaluable to our family.

I am delighted that Tate has been able to document the wealth of experience and extensive learning that his family has accumulated over decades to produce this book, which will no doubt serve as a significant source of education for many."

—DIANA "DINI" CECIL PICKERING, Great-Granddaughter of George W. Vanderbilt. Dini is Vice Chairperson of the Board of Directors for The Biltmore Company, which owns and operates Biltmore in Asheville, NC. Biltmore is the private estate of the late George W. Vanderbilt. Dini serves as the Family Office Director and oversees family business initiatives such as family planning meetings and training for future generations. She is also Chairperson of Biltmore's Corporate Philanthropy program. Dini is a sought-after speaker on the topic of family business, having presented for numerous conferences and board meetings.

"This is a very human book, and the best book on life insurance and ILITs that I have read. It's worth reading several times over. I highly recommend it!"

—THE LATE MICHAEL D. WEINBERG, JD, AEP©,
President, The Weinberg Group, Inc.

"I sat down and read Tate's book this morning, and it is excellent! Tate made a complex subject accessible and enjoyable with all of the wonderful and heartfelt stories. I desperately wish I had read this book 25 years ago, when we were putting together my mother's irrevocable life insurance trust. I was young, did not understand what was happening, and did not even know what questions to ask. Unfortunately, the attorney made some mistakes with the Crummey notices, which later caused us great stress and expense. Had I read ...*the Best Policy* I would have been able to avoid all of that frustration and pain. If you're involved in any way with life insurance, you absolutely need to read this book (and give it to your clients)."

—JOHN SPENCE, one of the top 100 business thought leaders in America in the area of trustworthy business behavior

---

"Our century-old business chartered a private trust company in 2012 to support the continued longevity of our family enterprise. That trust company has become responsible for a number of irrevocable life insurance trusts.

This book by Tate Groome is a superb and timely contribution to the growing knowledge requirements of both our Board of Directors and the operating leadership of our trust organization. I am grateful to the author for this effort to bring clarity to the issues surrounding the obligations we have taken on in our quest to build our family company."

—JIM ETHIER, Chairman of the Board, Bush Brothers & Company

"I was thrilled to see that a book about insurance could be so informative, while simultaneously being so entertaining! Tate has done a great job merging the human element with technical data in this publication. It is a book that fiduciaries managing ILITs, as well as grantors & beneficiaries of trusts should read."

"Tate Groome's book, ...*the Best Policy*, zeros in on what professionals in the life insurance industry have long known: 'the process of designing and managing policies on an ongoing basis is a far more important decision than trying to pick the best policy.' Tate's book strikes an interesting balance in showing how life insurance policies work best. It requires both the specialized knowledge of these complex and opaque financial products and, with a product that is designed by its nature to span generations, the ongoing care for clients. The mix of personal stories and technical information in the book shows how this has played out over the last 65 years at Tate's firm, Colton Groome."

"This book connects the dots for everyone who is concerned (or advising those concerned) about their family, their wealth, and legacy. Tate's writing is not only very accessible, but also enables anyone to understand how the mindful use of insurance can be a vital tool to achieving your goals, family harmony, and planning that aligns with your values."

—DR. GREG MCCANN, Founder of McCann & Associates, Founder of Stetson University's Family Enterprise Center

---

"This thoughtful and well-organized book marks a new generation of resources for family businesses. Tate's experience in the field of life insurance is evident in his writing. He has woven the personal stories of his clients together beautifully to explain the concepts. It read more like a conversation over coffee rather than a lumbering book of insurance information. He not only understands the complicated issues, but has the ability to explain it in simple, unassuming prose. Tate is a real pro, working with his father and brother in the family business that has served the area for over fifty years. Tate's consideration and appreciation for family bonds leaps off the pages of this book, and his encouragements will inspire you to design your legacy, starting today!"

—CINDY CLARKE is the Executive Director of the University of North Carolina Asheville Family Business Forum since 2006. The Forum is a continuing education series designed to support family businesses and was established in 2001.

"In my work with business families I encounter the whole range of human emotions. Often I am referred by trusted advisors with clients who know what needs to be done, but who are resistant to dealing with mortality issues. One in 3 family businesses will pass successfully to the next generation of owners. Many of those that fail do so because of liquidity crises at the time of death of the owner. Nothing fills that gap quite like life insurance. Tate talks about the 'dreaded' subject with humor and insight. His personal stories add a depth to his writing that is often missing in technical books."

—ROBERT CALDWELL is the founder of Family Firm Resources LLC of Charlotte. He regularly consults with, speaks and teaches on the subject the human side of family owned business. Since 2001, Robert has been the Babcock Family Business Fellow in the Wake Forest University Schools of Business.

"Being in the financial services business for 40 years, I've read a ton of books. Tate Groome is so passionate about his message I knew the book would be awesome and I was correct. My interest was piqued instantly quickly as I read ...the Best Policy: Irrevocable Life Insurance Trusts: Getting to the Heart of the Matter. Having a story weaved into how important life insurance can be allows you to experience it through someone else's eyes. Tate did a great job of clarifying his message to the reader while keeping them intrigued until the end. A must-read coming from someone that has written 8 books and understands how important education helps people. A must-read for all!!!"

—GINA PELLEGRINI, Owner of Pellegrini Team Consulting & Strategic Coach® Coach

"Tate has demystified life insurance in a way that is practical and useful, yet insightful. His insights and experience will greatly assist you as you navigate the process."

"In reading ...*the Best Policy* I was struck by the thoughtful stories that made the financial products understandable to not only professionals in the field but understandable to me and to the families I work with who must make the ultimate and educated decision of what to have in place when they are no longer here. Never an easy discussion but one that must be had and revisited periodically as the years pass. I met Tate and his family years ago and I am continually impressed at their dedication to improving the knowledge base and processes available to their clients, the industry and complex families of wealth everywhere."

About the Book

WE'RE ALL FAMILIAR with the old adage: "Honesty is the best policy." The adage drove our ethics as children, and all too often, we lose sight of the best policy as adults. In *...the Best Policy*, G. Tate Groome works to guide fiduciaries to the irrevocable life insurance policy structure that is truly right for their clients, deftly combining insurance expertise acquired over three generations with honesty and a code of conduct in an otherwise sterile business world. With a gentle emphasis on the personal, loving element that lies behind each policy, Groome uses *...the Best Policy* to help grantors and fiduciaries alike understand effective methods to monitor, manage, and sometimes restructure ILITs so that each grantor and trust beneficiary can have the *best* policy indeed.

...the Best Policy

Irrevocable Life Insurance Trusts: Getting to the Heart of the Matter

Second Edition

G. TATE GROOME, CFP®, CLU®, AEP®

LIFETRUST3D, LLC
Asheville, NC

Printed in the United States of America

Second Edition, Revised for 2020 Printing

Redwood Publishing, LLC
Orange County, California
www.redwooddigitalpublishing.com
info@redwooddigitalpublishing.com

ISBN: 978-1-952106-19-4 (paperback)
ISBN: 978-1-952106-20-0 (e-book)

Library of Congress Control Number: 2020902515

Disclaimer: Although the author and publisher have made every effort to ensure that the information in this book was correct at press time, the author and publisher do not assume and hereby disclaim any liability to any party for any loss, damage, or disruption caused by errors or omissions, whether such errors or omissions result from negligence, accident, or any other cause. This book is designed to provide information and motivation to its readers. It is sold with the understanding that the author and publisher are not engaged to render any type of psychological, legal, or any other kind of professional advice. The content of each article is the sole expression and opinion of its author and is not meant to substitute for any advice from your healthcare professionals, lawyers, therapists, business advisors/partners, or personal connections.

Cover Design by: Michelle Manley
Interior Layout by: Ghislain Viau

10 9 8 7 6 5 4 3 2 1

CONTENTS

Introduction to the Second Edition
Reviewing . . . *the Best Policy*

AS THE CEO of the nation's premier life insurance policy monitoring and consulting firm, my job is to help fiduciaries and policyholders ensure that they are maximizing benefits, reducing risk, and implementing best practices. At my company, LifeTrust3D™, due diligence is the backbone of our work. We monitor, so you can thrive.

I wrote and published the first edition of this book, *the Best Policy,* just five years ago. My goal is to help trustees, individuals, families, trust officers, fiduciaries and family offices understand how to use life insurance as a tool for providing financial security and peace of mind.

You'd think that not much could change in an industry in five short years, but we are encountering enormous— and ongoing—transformations in the field. The first edition of *the Best Policy* afforded me the opportunity to travel the country presenting at industry forums, college campuses, trust organizations and estate planning associations. Through my meetings with these industry leaders, trust professors, fiduciaries, and clients, it became clear to me the impact *the Best Policy* has had in multiple settings. However, like any meaningful asset, *the Best Policy* needed some thorough monitoring of its own to keep pace with industry changes. And so I offer you this second edition.

Whether you are a trust officer, student, estate planning attorney or leader of a trust company or family office, or are a consumer who wants to be certain that your family is protected, I want you to have the most up-to-date, accurate, unbiased information about what's really happening in the life insurance industry . . . so that you can come from a position of certainty and awareness.

In this second edition, I emphasize the following points:

- A sustained low-interest-rate environment continues to wreak havoc on insurance carriers and disrupt the status quo. What does this mean for policyholders? How will they be treated?
- Often overlooked maturity provisions are apt to cause unforeseen problems with estate planning. In a new chapter I tell you the story of a man who escaped Nazi Germany, became

an American success story, and then lost his life insurance because of a hidden contractual provision in his policy.

- With stock markets at all-time highs—but still volatile—more investor groups are looking for assets that don't correlate to markets. Life settlements, the purchase of existing life insurance policies by accredited third party investors, is an option that cannot be ignored for policies that may lapse or are no longer necessary. The demand by investors now outweighs the supply of policies available for purchase. Why have life settlements gained such buzz?

- Faced with increased sales pressure in an industry that has had decreasing overall sales, insurance carriers continue to design new policy types for the marketplace. Some are built to stand the test of time and others certainly are not. Choose wisely.

- With all the noise, how can consumers feel confident in their life insurance portfolios?

Some things haven't changed: When cared for properly, life insurance is still the one financial asset that protects families, closely held businesses, and legacies that took lifetimes to build by providing liquidity at the exact time it is most needed. There has never been a time when trusted life insurance advice has been more necessary than it is today. If you serve your clients in a fiduciary capacity, they need you more today than perhaps ever before. Life insurance issues continue to be ignored by the general public, but it remains the one asset that can make an immediate impact in beneficiaries' lives. It is up to fiduciaries—those who care enough to bring up the issues raised in this book—to make sure their clients have … *the Best Policy*.

What you'll learn in these pages will give you the ability to better advise and protect your clients. Thank you for reading, for your support, and for the opportunity to be of service.

Tate Groome
2020

1

Origins

MY JOURNEY IN the life insurance industry began on Halloween night in 1960. (Stay with me, now—I was born in 1979, but my story began before my parents even dreamed me up.) My then eight-year-old father, George, was out trick-or-treating when he spotted another young boy in a ghost costume. The "ghost" kept tripping over the hem of his costume—and candy went flying everywhere. George stopped his trick-or-treating, helped the boy to his feet, collected his candy, and then they went on together to the next house. Despite George's efforts, his new friend kept falling. After the fourth time the ghost tripped, George finally asked the other boy his name. "Walter," the ghost said, grateful that George continued to help him while the other kids just passed him by.

Little did young George know that his small act of kindness that Halloween night would change his life—and that the ripple effect it produced would influence mine. Young George Groome and Walter Colton quickly became friends. Once brought together, the two were inseparable. They remained friends through adulthood, rooming together during college at the University of North Carolina at Chapel Hill. (Go Heels!)

My father's story is a riches-to-rags then back-to-riches story. George was the youngest of five children, and his father, W. J., had a lucrative job at the Pepsi-Cola Bottling Company. When my father was eight, W. J. lost his job at Pepsi. Serendipitously, George met young Walter around the same time, and he started spending a lot of his time at the Colton house.

Young George's life was very different from the lives of his older siblings. Reluctant to talk about his childhood, my father often jokes that he spent so much time at the Coltons' because he just liked hanging out with Walter's three sisters! He doesn't mention the mansion he grew up in—or the two full-time housekeepers who worked there—before they lost everything when he was only eight years old. He doesn't like to tell us about having to work at a local factory during high school, sweeping glass on the night shift, to help support their household. He doesn't talk about the many nights he spent at the laundromat with his mom, or the time he stood up to his father when W.J. was in an alcohol-induced rage. Although I can't blame him for loving the Colton girls as a teenager, I know the real reason he spent so much time there was because they made him feel like family.

Tradition was important to the Colton family, and in keeping with tradition they always went to Henry Colton's office on the fifteenth floor of the BB&T building in downtown Asheville, North Carolina, to watch the Christmas parade. George was always included. During Thanksgiving of 1972, as my father was nearing the end of his college career at UNC's business school, that tradition of watching the Christmas parade turned into much more. When the parade ended, everyone went his or her own way except for George and Henry, who sat quietly gazing over downtown and the beautiful Blue Ridge Mountains beyond it. George said to Henry, "I don't know exactly what you do, Mr. Colton, but I know it has something to do with finance. I know you're well respected and successful, and that you always seem to have a smile on your face. I want to be just like you. Can I come work with you after graduation?"

With his own son Walter pursuing a career in international business, Henry had already considered hiring George to help continue the family business. A brilliant student, George was not only highly qualified, but had the necessary motivation to succeed in a demanding business. Henry knew he could count on young George to make his way in the financial business and do it the "right way," which, to Henry, was "his way." The two looked at each other thoughtfully, and after a moment, Henry said, "Of course."

That first chance encounter, trick-or-treating in 1960, led to my father dedicating his life to the wealth management and insurance protection industry. Dad went to work for Mr. Colton after his final exam, and the company began to evolve into the incredible organization it now is. Henry Colton's impact on my father's life shaped *my* life before I even understood how important it truly was. The name of the firm today, Colton Groome Insurance Advisors, Inc., pays homage to the man who first planted the seed for my father's career . . . and for mine.

Before I was drawn to my father's career, I followed in my mother's footsteps, becoming a teacher in an inner-city school system after graduating from college. I started in an at-risk elementary school, where I coached the middle school basketball team.

I loved the impact I was able to make on other people's lives as a teacher and coach, but I eventually realized how badly I wanted to learn about the business world. Who better to teach me than my father, the very best man—and professional—I'd ever been around? He was in the prime of his career at the time, and I realized what a rare opportunity I had to learn from someone so experienced and educated. My other option, of course, would have been to go back to school for business, but I believed (and still believe) that a person can earn a master's degree from an educational institution or a PhD in life experience. I chose the latter, and, from then on, I attended the "George Groome School of Business" every day.

So many businesspeople of my generation want to follow the investment manager track and work on Wall Street or the hedge fund industry. After observing and working with my father, I knew I didn't want to manage money like everyone else. I wanted to protect families. My personal story shows how important families and multigenerational legacies can be. I want everyone out there to protect their legacies—not just for today, but for generations to come.

From L to R: Tate Groome, Matt Groome, Henry Colton, George Groome

2

How $22 Million Changed *My* Life... Not Just the Beneficiary's

"EVERYONE WAS LAUGHING," Charles said. I waited for him to say more.

Charles, a former real estate developer, had purchased a $10 million whole life insurance policy years ago from another agent who was now retired. Charles was a family friend and a client of ours, but I knew his financial situation was in flux. I called him one morning when he had just returned from a family vacation and asked if I could meet with him to review the policy he'd recently mentioned to me in passing. (He had received a notice from the insurance carrier that the premium would be increasing significantly.) When I asked to schedule a meeting, Charles replied, "How soon can you be at my office?"

Puzzled by how quickly he wanted to meet with me, I told him I'd be there in fifteen minutes. I scrambled to prepare and rushed across town to his office.

Charles briefed me on his situation. He had accumulated significant debt on a large real estate project. The project would eventually turn out to be quite profitable, but I knew he needed to increase his life insurance to provide his family with a greater degree of financial security, and to allow his real estate brilliance ample time to flourish. Life insurance is the one financial tool that allows a person to dial in on the end game.

> The end game is the financial position a breadwinner would have provided for their loved ones if he or she had lived long enough to do so.

In the unfortunate event one is not alive to reach the end game, life insurance is the only self-completing financial tool in our industry.

Charles's initial goal had been to make sure that his family would always be able to maintain its standard of living, even if he wasn't there as the provider. He didn't want his survivors to inherit any of his debt. His new real estate investment had raised the financial stakes as well as the pressure on Charles. He knew it would be a success, but it was so dynamic, no one could get it to the finish line except Charles.

As I sank into a deep, brown leather chair in his boardroom, Charles said again, "Everyone was laughing." He smiled. He described a recent family vacation at the beach. He told me about the perfect ocean breeze and the soothing sound of the waves washing up on the shore. Seated in a beach chair, he had held his wife's hand and basked in the sheer joy of listening to his four grandchildren playing in the sand. "I closed my eyes and heard my grandkids laugh," he told me, "and I just never want to worry that they won't laugh again."

Charles called me to his office because he was ready to expand his life insurance policy. Charles had decided long ago that owning life insurance inside an irrevocable trust wasn't right for him—as the head of a real estate empire, he wanted to maintain outright, unfettered control of the cash value he had accumulated within his whole life policy.

The estate planning benefits of owning life insurance in an irrevocable trust are plentiful. *Irrevocable* means "not able to be changed, reversed, or recovered. Final." Once a policy is owned in an irrevocable trust, it is managed by a trustee who makes decisions based on the values and directives of the grantor, or maker of the trust. In most states, it is difficult or impossible for a grantor to access the accumulated cash in their funds. (I delve deeper into the mechanics of an irrevocable trust in chapter 3.)

Charles and I sat in that boardroom for almost two hours that day, and together we designed *his* insurance plan: one that would meet his goals and needs for that day as well as the rest of his life. I'm sharing Charles's story because it brings up an important point about life insurance. Life is constantly changing. A client's hopes and dreams change and evolve. Money doesn't necessarily provide happiness, but it will absolutely allow for certain freedoms. Clients buy life insurance because they love their families. Whether it's the oldest member of the family or a newly married couple wanting to make sure they can take care of their loved ones, the biggest motivator to purchase life insurance is love. In so many words, Charles told me something I hear most of my clients say: "I love my family, and one of the best ways I can take care of them is to look out for everyone financially. And one of the best ways I can do that is to ensure that they won't have to take on my debts, and that a reliable reserve is here for them when I go."

One of the biggest conundrums with *any* life insurance portfolio lies in balancing premiums and current finances with the ultimate value of the policy. Many people purchased policies back in the late 1980s and 1990s, when the estate tax exemption was *significantly* lower than it is today. In addition, interest rates were much higher back then than they have been in the last decade. Depending on the policy design and structure, these factors could lead to premiums increasing or being funded longer than anticipated. Policies underperforming original expectations combined with the increased estate tax exemption leave some families no longer needing as much life insurance as they once did. Perhaps they need a different type of coverage or need it for a certain period of time (like Charles did in order to leverage a significant real estate project). In some situations—even in a booming economy—grantors may no longer be able to afford a premium amount that may have felt insignificant during their working years. Maybe their goals have simply changed, or perhaps the beneficiaries need access to some of the cash value for emergencies.

Life changes. Economic times change. Political environments and tax laws change. Insurance performance and products change. Change is inevitable. It is crucial to make sure clients' insurance programs continue to meet their goals and premium tolerance today. People often think that life insurance is a static financial vehicle, but nothing could be further from the truth. Owning life insurance inside an irrevocable trust adds yet another layer of complexity—as if life insurance weren't already complex enough. Life insurance is dynamic. With its moving parts, it should be monitored similarly to an investment account. The policy that best serves a client needs to be properly structured

The biggest motivator to purchase life insurance is love. People often think that life insurance is a very static financial vehicle, but nothing could be farther from the truth. All life insurance is incredibly dynamic, with many moving parts, and it has to be managed that way.

and managed while still being flexible enough to allow for change.

To create the *best* policy for a client, we have to go back and ask the question that we so often asked as children: *Why?* Why did we buy life insurance in the first place? Why do we maintain it?

To effectively manage your clients' life insurance policies, take a step back. Start with *why*, and then keep asking as time passes. "Why are you purchasing a life insurance policy?" you might ask a client. "What are your goals for your policy *today*—to protect your wealth or protect yourself from debt? To provide an inheritance? To leverage your existing assets? To minimize tax implications? To provide for your favorite charity? How do we make the most efficient use of your assets? How can we maximize benefit for the trust and for the trust beneficiaries?" Sometimes the goal is simply to reduce risk for a policy that's not performing as planned or that could lapse. Life insurance is all part of a bigger plan, and it must be consistently reevaluated as life changes.

> To effectively manage your clients' life insurance policies, take a step back... sometimes the goal is simply to reduce risk for a policy that's not performing well or could lapse. Life insurance is all part of a bigger plan, and it must be consistently reevaluated as life changes.

Have you ever heard of the classic Chinese Bamboo Tree parable? I first heard it in a church sermon when I was just starting to write the first edition of my book. It spoke to me profoundly, and I knew it had a place in … *the Best Policy*. Here it goes: You take a little seed, plant it, water it, and fertilize it for a whole year—and nothing happens.

You water and fertilize the seed for a second year. Nothing.

A third year of caring for the plant passes—nothing. You water and fertilize for a fourth year—*still* nothing.

You water and fertilize for a fifth year. Sometime during the fifth year, finally, gratifyingly, the Chinese bamboo tree sprouts . . . and grows ninety feet in ninety days!

Nourishing and reaping the benefits of a trust-owned life insurance policy is like growing that bamboo. During those first five years, you don't necessarily see any progress above ground, but the root system is establishing itself as a solid foundation for the future. Over the course of five years, it spreads and deepens in preparation for the dramatic growth ahead—and when it is finally time, the beautiful plant bursts through the soil and surpasses expectations because it was cared for properly.

Many consumers consider the purchase of life insurance the ultimate goal and figure that once they've purchased it, it will take care of itself. They work and work, trying to find *the* right policy, going through underwriting and jumping through all the various hoops necessary to purchase a policy—and it gets even more complicated when the policy is purchased within a trust. Once consumers find and buy that policy, they think, *That's it. I'm done. I've taken care of the work, and I don't need to do anything else.*

I learned from my father that the **policy purchase is not the end game—it's just the beginning**. The policy has to be nurtured for a long, long time. We need to make sure that its roots are established and strong, and we need to pay attention to environmental changes so we know when we're watering it too much or not fertilizing enough (i.e., putting too much premium in or not funding the policy enough).

The ultimate benefits to life insurance are numerous: estate planning, charitable giving, family protection, business succession, inheritance, and so on. The real key to owning a policy, though, is monitoring and managing what you have so that you and the beneficiaries *can* reap those benefits. A homeowner can't buy a house and then never make any repairs or adjustments. In the same way, a client shouldn't invest in a policy and then never adjust.

After agents sell a policy, technically they are under no contractual obligation to manage it; they've received their commission and are ready to move on. Recent statistics show that 70 percent of life insurance policies are orphaned, meaning they no longer have an assigned agent. Insureds on orphaned policies are left to navigate insurance carriers, 1-800 land, and complex products on their own. Unmonitored policies may lead to significant issues for clients. Most critically we see issues arise just at the moment when a family is least able to handle them. Increased premiums never come at opportune times. This may lead to a life insurance death benefit that is less than the client initially desired. I've witnessed situations where grieving widows and children discover that their husband or father—faced with a large premium increase—decided to allow a term

> Leaving a policy
> without active and
> routine monitoring
> is like leaving your
> Chinese bamboo
> tree without water.
> You can't reap the
> benefits if you don't
> routinely nourish the
> foundation.

rider to drop off the policy, resulting in a decreased death benefit for his beneficiaries. Leaving a policy without active and routine monitoring is like leaving your Chinese bamboo tree without water. You can't reap the benefits if you don't routinely nourish the foundation.

As a fresh-faced man in my late twenties, I was surprised when Charles trusted me enough to go beyond a typical client-advisor relationship and confide in me. He was a big, intimidating man even in his later years; he *looked* like a powerful businessman. He was a true mogul in the Carolina real estate world. I certainly didn't anticipate that he would put such faith in a young guy like me, much less that he would purchase millions of dollars' worth of life insurance from me. But Charles trusted me because I spent time with him. We developed a deep relationship that lasted beyond our sales conversations. I learned of his greatest joys and sorrows, his fears, his relationship with his father—all intimacies that I'd never expected (nor thought I deserved) to gain with this titan. In return, I told Charles about the challenges I was facing as a young father of two children at the time. My daughter was sick in the hospital. Our medical bills were piling up.

Charles was an excellent judge of character, and he saw something in me that allowed him to trust me deeply—maybe he saw a part of himself in me—and that trust allowed me to move forward confidently in my career. I thought if I earned Charles' trust, I didn't need to be intimated to approach anyone. This is a gift for which I will be forever grateful.

After Charles and I had been working for some time to reengineer his insurance plan, I realized that we would be able to reduce his six-figure premium while simultaneously increasing the death benefit from $10 million to $22 million. This was in the day when almost any well-funded whole life contract could be exchanged for universal life with secondary guarantees, an eliminated or reduced premium, and increased death benefit. Oh, the good old days! If you are in the insurance business, you know such policy exchanges are few and far between in today's environment. Reducing his premium allowed Charles to secure an additional $10 million ten-year term life insurance policy to protect his family while the real estate debt mounted up. He knew the debt would only exist for a shorter period of time; thus, a ten-year term made perfect sense. He now increased his coverage by $12 million for roughly the same premium he had been paying for his $10 million whole life policy.

Unfortunately, Charles was right to be concerned. The real estate debt existed for only three years, but it weighed on him heavily. Although it was diminishing as planned, Charles didn't make it to see the end game. Sadly, he passed away only three years after we increased his life insurance—but the seed that we planted and nourished together sprouted during those years. In the face of tragedy, being prepared gave Charles comfort in his final days.

Shortly after Charles's death, I knocked on his daughter Hillary's door. She greeted me warmly as her kids chased each other in the hallway behind her. I gave her a big hug and then handed her an envelope. As a single mother, Hillary had been supporting her children on her own, and fortunately Charles had been able to make gifts to her during his lifetime. At my initial meetings with Charles, as I sat in that brown leather chair, he had explained to me that Hillary would need financial help if he wasn't here to support her. Together, Charles and I had come up with a solution.

Hillary eyed the envelope curiously, then looked back at me. I nodded encouragingly, and she slowly opened the envelope. She pulled out the enclosed paper and stared, in disbelief and then shock, at a check for $2 million made out in her name.

Charles's widow was the beneficiary of the first $20 million. Charles and I had designed his policy this way largely to pay off his real estate debt. Our intention was also to provide income for the next thirty-plus years so the love of his life could live comfortably, the way she would have were her husband still living. With some thoughtful and careful life insurance plan design, though, Charles and I were able to increase the death benefit from $20 million to $22 million, leaving an extra $2 million for Hillary.

Check in hand, an astonished Hillary looked back up at me—and burst into tears. Hillary had been under the impression that her father's life insurance would be used primarily to pay off his debt and benefit her mother, and she'd had no idea that anything significant was coming to her. "You don't know what this means to me," she told me through her sobs of relief. "You do not know what this means to me."

That extra $2 million made a world of difference for Hillary. It allowed her to care for her children as a single mother in the way that she so badly wanted to, and in the manner that Charles had imagined had he been there to provide for Hillary himself. I have learned in my career that money—or, more specifically, money issuing from life insurance proceeds—gives families and beneficiaries financial freedom at the time when they most desperately need it. It is the end game planning tool.

That weighty but gratifying moment with Hillary has stayed with me. I saw how much difference a life insurance policy could make in a family's life. After surviving grief and loss, beneficiaries can be handed the smallest piece of paper and know, without a doubt, that they were loved and cared for.

Charles was a real estate developer, so liquidity was vital to his business, and he had determined early on that he didn't want a trust to own his life insurance (or the cash value that he'd accumulated within the policies). However, an irrevocable trust is an incredibly powerful planning tool that, managed correctly, can cement one's legacy for years to come.

Had we made the decision to use one, we likely could have made postmortem planning for Charles's surviving spouse less complex. Charles desired control during his lifetime over the policies, which trumped estate tax issues. As my father always says, "Money in times of no agreements is better than agreements in times of no money." In other words, it was better in this situation to let him do what he thought was best, because pushing him toward a planning technique he wasn't comfortable with might have jeopardized his having life insurance at all.

Now, a decade after Charles's passing, I often wonder how the ripple effect of his life insurance proceeds will continue to affect his loved ones. Charles's family and I have been able to maintain a warm and caring relationship—I see his wife often, and I see Hillary and her children frequently as well. They're all still laughing, and I know Charles hears them.

3

The Irrevocable Life Insurance Trust:
A Practical Overview

THE IRREVOCABLE LIFE insurance trust (or ILIT) is one of the most powerful estate planning tools ever created. When managed correctly, this incredibly potent tool can secure one's legacy for years to come. However, ILITs are often undermanaged and overlooked. The notion that ILIT-owned life insurance is a static wealth-transfer vehicle could not be farther from the truth. Both ILITs and the life insurance policies they own are incredibly dynamic and need to be managed accordingly.

The word *irrevocable* turns off some people (like my client Charles, described in chapter 2), but the true meaning is simply that the terms of the trust generally can't be changed by the grantor (the creator of the trust). *Changed*, however, is very different in this context from *managed*, and by investing in a trustee who maintains the policy properly, a client can benefit greatly.

There are many reasons an ILIT is a great option, but the main one is that it protects clients from the federal estate tax. The estate tax is subject to the political leanings in Washington, DC. As of 2019, it taxes an estate at 40 percent of its value over and above the estate tax exemption amount. Twenty years ago, individuals were exempt from the tax for estates valued at or under $650,000. In 2019, the exemption amount is $11.4 million per person, or $22.8 million per couple. During the Obama administration, the exemption was $5 million per person, indexed for inflation. The exemption level will most likely continue to change depending on which political party dominates Washington.

Life insurance is not subject to income taxes when owned properly, but it *is* considered part of one's taxable estate if the policy is owned personally or by a business owned by the insured. Life insurance proceeds can sometimes send the value of an estate north of the exemption limit, thus subjecting that individual to the estate tax. When life insurance is owned in an irrevocable trust—and the administration requirements of that ILIT are met— life insurance proceeds retain not only their income tax advantages, but are also received free of estate tax.

Here's how an ILIT works: A grantor works with an attorney to create an irrevocable trust that meets the grantor's long-term goals. The trust dictates how proceeds are to be paid out (lump sum, stream of payments, or managed inside the trust for future generations) and to whom (aka the beneficiaries). The grantor names a trustee who then works with an insurance advisor to acquire life insurance on behalf of the trust. Typically, the trustee is a trust company, trust officer within a bank, attorney, or CPA, but can also be a family member—someone who understands trust law and can manage the steps required to qualify as irrevocable. By using a properly structured ILIT, grantors can leverage their trust and purchase a significant asset (life insurance) without it being subject to estate taxes. By protecting the life insurance policy from taxation, the grantor guarantees that surviving loved ones will have access to the liquidity they need to survive.

> By using a properly structured ILIT, grantors can leverage their trust and purchase a significant asset (life insurance) without it being subject to estate taxes, thereby providing the necessary liquidity for their loved ones.

Throughout their life, grantors can make annual present-interest gifts to the trust that can be used to pay the annual premium as well as any necessary trust fees. Because the trust is set up to benefit beneficiaries, payments to the trust are considered a gift to family members and are thus tax-free up to a value of $15,000 per beneficiary per person. This means a married couple can gift $30,000 total annually ($15,000 each) to each of their children, grandchildren, or anyone they choose. These gifts are called Crummey gifts—not because they're bad (apologies for the dad joke). Clifford Crummey was the first person to use these gifts in the 1960s.

To better understand how an ILIT works, consider this example. Mr. and Mrs. Blane ran a farm with an estate valued at $5 million. Like most farmers, the Blanes didn't have significant liquidity; their land and machinery made up the bulk of their worth, and they continually reinvested in the farm. In 2003, the Blanes died in a car accident. At the time, the estate tax exemption was $1 million per person or $2 million per couple. Suddenly, the Blanes' grieving children faced a terrible situation. Their parents were gone and they had an estate worth $5 million—a full $3 million over the exemption level. Given the estate tax law, the Blanes' kids owed 40 percent of that value to the government: $1.2 million. Fortunately, the Blanes had an ILIT with a policy worth $1 million. Because the policy was not counted as part of their estate, it did not increase

THE IRREVOCABLE LIFE INSURANCE TRUST

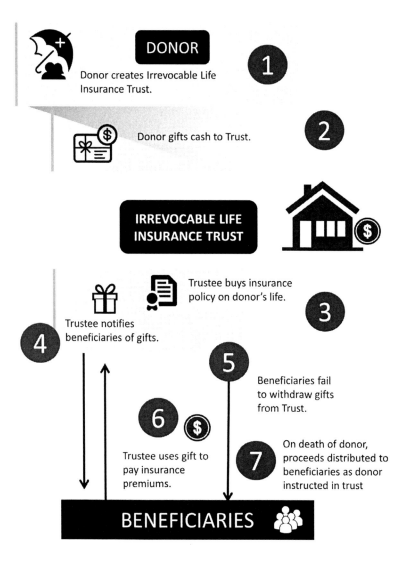

DONOR

Donor creates Irrevocable Life Insurance Trust.

1

Donor gifts cash to Trust.

2

IRREVOCABLE LIFE INSURANCE TRUST

Trustee buys insurance policy on donor's life.

3

Trustee notifies beneficiaries of gifts.

4

Beneficiaries fail to withdraw gifts from Trust.

5

Trustee uses gift to pay insurance premiums.

6

On death of donor, proceeds distributed to beneficiaries as donor instructed in trust

7

BENEFICIARIES

the amount of estate taxes owed. The full amount of $1 million was received free of both income and estate taxes. The Blane kids used the policy to pay the majority of the federal estate tax. If they hadn't had the policy in trust, the Blanes would have had to sell off part of the farm to pay taxes. They would not only have lost their parents— they would have lost their parents' legacy. Today the farm remains in the Blane family.

When I released the first edition of this book in 2015, the federal estate tax exemption was $5,430,000 per person or $10,860,000 per couple. The Tax Cuts and Jobs Act of 2017 increased the estate tax exemption to $11,180,000 per person indexed annually through the year 2025. At that point, it is scheduled to revert to $5 million per person (as of 2019, the exemption is $11,400,000 per person).

Once thing is certain: The estate tax exemption is a moving target. Many grantors who have a combined estate under $22,800,000 in 2019 may believe they no longer need an ILIT, but we know that estate tax laws change depending on the political landscape. Just because the exemption exceeds an estate's value does not mean it's advisable to abandon an irrevocable trust.

As an example of why you can't rely on the current exemption for future planning, imagine a married couple: Each partner is seventy-five years old in 2019. Together, they have a current net worth of $15 million. They allow their life insurance policy to lapse based on the current estate tax exemption. What happens if the estate tax minimum reverts back to $5 million ($10 million per couple) as planned in 2026? They will be eighty-two years old and have a potential estate tax exposure of $5 million. Do you know how hard it is to obtain life insurance when you are eighty-two? It's possible, but it costs a lot of money.

Aside from protecting assets from estate laws, there are other important benefits to the ILIT. Grantors can embed values inside the provisions of a trust. One couple I worked with set up a trust to pay distributions to their children if they chose rewarding but low-paying careers. They said they would match a salary dollar for dollar if their children opted for something service-oriented—say, teaching or the ministry.

Another advantage of the ILIT is that it may also help protect assets from divorce, undue influence, bad decisions, and creditors. Due to more progressive trust laws that include "dynasty" language, certain states, such as Alaska, Tennessee, Nevada, South Dakota, and Delaware, offer favorable trust provisions that may allow the grantor greater asset protection, and flexibility, and may enable wealth to be protected for future generations.

Each ILIT is unique and should be customized to the grantor's goals. The key to using an irrevocable life insurance trust to a client's advantage lies in managing the trust and its assets prudently. During this time of uncertainty, flexibility is paramount.

One situation that ILIT trustees have now become all too familiar with is when a grantor calls wanting to discontinue premium gifts. Perhaps their financial circumstances have changed; or they feel they don't need as much life insurance due to the increased estate tax exemption; or they simply no longer have the desire or wherewithal to continue funding premium gifts. The trustee is then placed in a difficult situation: they have a duty to provide the maximum possible benefit to the trust beneficiaries, but are reliant upon the trust's grantor to provide the funding. Trustees often are stuck between a rock and a hard place.

We find that without proper education, trustees may not be aware of more favorable alternatives than simply allowing life insurance policies to be surrendered for cash value or lapse without value. In fact, LifeTrust3D™ has a documented Policy Surrender Protocol™ to help Trustees evaluate all viable alternatives prior to a policy surrender or lapse. Recognizing trustees have a duty of loyalty to the trust beneficiaries, here are a few alternatives that may prove prudent to not only consider, but as proper file documentation:

1. **Communicate**: Communicate with Trust Beneficiaries: the first step in determining viable alternatives is to communicate with the Trust Beneficiaries. Be certain they understand the Grantors no longer desire to make premium gifts. Depending on the trust language and financial circumstances of the beneficiaries, they may have the wherewithal to make contributions to the trust so the current life insurance can be continued. Although it is rare for a beneficiary to step up and make contributions, it makes them aware that changes are on the horizon.

2. **Premium Flexibility**: Determine whether a policy's premiums can be skipped or reduced, and how that would impact the policy's long-term viability. Depending on the client's age the policy's cost structure, it may be possible to delay the decision to discontinue life insurance without a significant impact to the policy's cash value.

3. **Death Benefit Reduction**: Consider a death benefit reduction as opposed to outright policy surrender. For example, whole life may offer a reduced, paid-up death benefit option that may have merit.

4. **Consider using term insurance**: In fact, uncertainty is just the place for relatively inexpensive but convertible term insurance. Convertible term insurance allows insureds to lock in their insurability today with the ability to convert to permanent insurance in the future with no medical underwriting. Note, purchasing convertible term insurance is not as simple as it sounds. Be sure to consult with an independent insurance advisor who understands the differences among term carriers in regard to conversion privileges.

5. **1035 Tax-Free Policy Exchange**: for insured's in favorable health, a 1035 exchange may provide a greater life insurance benefit with $0 on-going premium than reduced death benefit options available with the current policy. For policy's with taxable gains upon surrender, this alternative may provide also alleviate the trust from undesirable income tax implications.

6. **Life Settlement**: as opposed to an outright surrender for the policy's cash surrender value, a life settlement, in the right set of circumstances my provide significantly greater value to the trust than a policy surrender. Learn more about Life Settlements in Chapter 9. In addition, the Tax Cuts

and Jobs Act provides favorable tax treatment of life settlements.

When considering a policy surrender, be certain to understand tax implications especially if there is a gain in the contract. Who will be responsible for any taxes due? Is the trust a Grantor or Non-Grantor Trust? Regardless of the outcome, exploring all viable alternatives is prudent and indeed, the best policy.

4

Who's in the Cockpit, Anyway? Why a Prudent Process Matters Now More than Ever

IF YOU'VE EVER traveled far, you're probably familiar with the grueling routine of getting on an airplane. You drag yourself through check-in and airport security, make your way to the gate, wait for another forty-five minutes, and finally are allowed to board the plane. During takeoff, you fall asleep, sure that the hardest part of your travel is over now that you are in the air.

Can you imagine waking up midflight to find that no one is in the cockpit, and you have no way to take control of the plane? Sure, that scenario is a bit outlandish, but it's exactly what the owners and beneficiaries of many life insurance policies are facing today.

Safely arriving at your destination requires prudent planning. If we think of an ILIT in the estate-planning context as a vehicle to accomplish plans for the client, it can be likened to a long flight that transfers estate assets to a specified destination—the intended beneficiaries. Numerous parties are involved in the preflight planning, yet the ultimate success of the flight relies on the expertise of the pilot flying the plane.

Unfortunately, a disturbing trend threatens to undermine the best-laid plans: the sudden disappearance of a pilot soon after the journey has begun. The traditional compensation structure for insurance agents doesn't directly incentivize them to stay in the cockpit to ensure a safe landing. Many agents retire or change careers after selling policies, or are not committed to prudent policy-serve standards.

When life insurance policies are abandoned by those who are supposed to be monitoring them and ensuring that they stay on course over time, irreparable harm will be done to the policies' performance—and eventually, to the beneficiaries. The insurance advisors who are committed to their policyholders enjoy long and rewarding careers in the insurance industry.

A Different Kind of Asset

In the management of a client's investment assets, active monitoring and reporting are now the standard. Assets should be reviewed periodically and rebalanced and adjusted based on performance, economic considerations, and the client's goals and objectives. The consequences of an underperforming investment portfolio aren't typically dire, and there are myriad ways to take corrective action. Underperformance in a life insurance policy, though, can drastically alter its intended course, making options for corrective action limited once the damage has been done.

Life insurance policies purchased to provide long-term death benefits often span multiple decades. Few other assets owned as widely as life insurance last as long or have such material financial impact on beneficiaries. Life insurance is generally more rigid than other financial instruments due to financial, health-related, or tax-related barriers to entry and exit. Thus, life insurance requires an

> Life insurance is generally more rigid than other financial instruments due to financial, health-related, or tax-related barriers to entry and exit. Thus, life insurance requires an uncommon combination of due diligence up front, policy preplanning, monitoring, and adaptation and flexibility within a sometimes confining set of boundaries.

uncommon combination of due diligence up front, policy preplanning, monitoring, and adaptation and flexibility within a sometimes confining set of boundaries.

Some of you will be well acquainted with the requirements of managing a trust investment portfolio. The table on the following page points out the key differences between investment management and ILIT management.

Flying through a Turbulence Zone

When it comes to pre-purchase product research, consumers' knowledge has increased tremendously in the last decade. Much has been written about the selection and structure of life insurance policies, and in the age of the Internet, most of this material is very accessible. Professional continuing education sessions on life insurance are widely available as well. As such, at least one of a client's professional advisors (attorney, trustee, financial advisor, or accountant) is likely to have *some* exposure to the life insurance acquisition process, and they'll typically assist in the purchasing process to some degree. Unfortunately, this tends to be where the practical assistance ends, and the policy owner is often left alone with a strange and complicated asset.

The problem with this approach is that **risks are most prevalent *after* policy purchase**. Prior to purchase,

Trust Investment Portfolio	ILIT Life Insurance Policy
Under-performance results in lower portfolio balances.	Under-performance may result in loss of the entire policy and may have tax implications.
Near limitless investment options and strategies to recover from portfolio underperformance including: change allocations, find lower fees, change managers, change durations, add more money, or increase risk exposure.	Investment choices (if any) and options to recover are dictated by the type of policy, policy funding limits, and other factors. It may not be possible to change allocations, lower fees, add money, change durations or alter the risk exposure.
Easy to quantify cost to put an investment strategy back on track.	May be difficult or even impossible to quantify the ultimate cost to put a life insurance strategy back on track.
An investment portfolio might have lower expense levels over time as the asset base grows.	Many policies have significantly escalating expenses over time.
It is simple to change the risk portfolio or time horizon of an investment portfolio.	A policy may not allow a change in the investment risk profile or the investment time horizon.
Borrowing or distributions from an investment portfolio can be easily quantified and modeled under a variety of assumptions and fact patterns.	The full impact of a loan, partial surrender or distribution from a life insurance policy may not be easily determined prior to execution or even disclosed in some policy types.
Relatively easy to diversify a portfolio at any time without inordinate increases in associated expenses.	Available underwriting offers and product types may result in significantly higher costs for carrier diversification and is available up front only.
The trustee may unilaterally choose to liquidate one or more investment positions.	While a trustee may surrender a policy outright, he may not execute a life settlement without consent of the insured.
There is significant breadth and depth of research and insight on investment strategies and portfolios.	Sound research and insight on life insurance policies is difficult to find. What information is out there is often plagued by omission or supposition of fact patterns or actions.
Many trustees are very knowledgeable on investments and investment strategies.	Few trustees are experts on life insurance.
Some investments may have barriers to exit such as income taxes, capital gains taxes, back end loads, surrender charge periods, notice requirements, or lock up periods.	A life insurance policy ahs barriers to exit that may include income taxes, surrender charges, forfeiture of earnings, notice requirements, lock up periods, and delays for receipt of surrender proceeds.
Some investments may have barriers to entry such as minimum investment requirements.	Life insurance policies have significant barriers to entry including willingness and consent of the insured party to undergo underwriting, health worthiness and the insured, a pricing structure that escalates with age, and restrictions on minimum and maximum allowable premiums.

i Two white papers are available for additional insight: 1) Repercussions of a Sustained Low Interest Rate Environment on Life Insurance Policies, and 2) A Matter of Choice which discusses life insurance company selection.
ii AL, AZ, DE, FL, NC, ND, OH, PA, SC, SD, TN, VA, and WY
iii Bove Jr., Alexander A (February 2014), The Death of the Trust, Trusts & Estates, 51-55
iv In re Stuart Cochran Irrevocable Trust, 901 N.E.2d 1128 (Indiana Court of Appeals, March 2, 2009)
v French v. Wachovia Bank, N.A., 2011 U.S. Dist. LEXIS 72808 (E.D. Wisconsin 2011)

© 2013 Valmark Advisers

great care is often taken to ensure a proper balance of carrier strength, diversification, policy funding, and policy ownership considerations. Undoubtedly, these factors warrant significant time and attention. But so many complications manifest after the policy has been issued, including the following:

> The problem is that risks are most prevalent after policy purchase. Prior to purchase, great care is taken to ensure a proper balance within ownership, but potential threats such as premium timing, change in beneficiaries, loan strategies, and more are all risks to the policy's ultimate success.

- premium timing and administrative risks
- change in policy ownership without regard to transfer for value issues
- testing violations such as Guideline Premium Test (GPT), Cash Value Accumulation Test (CVAT) or creating a Modified Endowment Contract (MEC)
- policy loans accruing on policies at interest rates as high as 8 percent

- expiration of term conversion rights
- maturity provisions not providing the substantial benefit once promised
- sudden cost of insurance increases by carriers
- termination of term policies
- underperformance due to lower-than-anticipated returns
- carrier changes, carriers going out of business, or carriers outsourcing calls to call centers that are not properly staffed

These are all real potential threats to the ultimate success and safe arrival of the policy's life insurance death benefit proceeds.

What happens if a plane is lacking expert guidance as it flies through a storm system? It may not get to the destination, the passengers may get hurt, and at the very least, it's going to be a turbulent, unpleasant flight. What, then, are the consequences if these risks to a policy manifest and aren't properly addressed over time?

The consequences may be financial in nature, and they may be less than obvious to the naked eye. The most apparent repercussions are increased out-of-pocket premium requirements, reductions in the death benefit, lower cash value, or loss of coverage prior to death. When these things go awry, there may be side effects too—for example, gift or income taxes may be incurred. Reducing or terminating coverage when the life insurance was a key foundation in a planning strategy could result in a wide range of consequences, such as the inability to properly transfer business interests, unequal estate distributions to heirs, lack of liquidity, or forced sales of assets that were never intended to be sold.

A life insurance policy, just like a plane, is affected by internal and external forces. The grantor of an irrevocable life insurance trust can't manage the policy. The insurance agent or broker, attorney, and accountant may have no legal or contractual duty after the policy's been sold, which should scare grantors and beneficiaries—a *lot*. So who, then, is sitting in the cockpit monitoring the policy and reacting to the external forces?

The burden rests solely in the hands of the trustee. Regardless of whether they are a corporate trustee, a professional trustee, or a family member, the trustee's role is to skillfully navigate harsh conditions so the policy may arrive safely at its desired destination . . . which may be thirty, forty, or even fifty years in the future. The Uniform Prudent Investors Act (UPIA) provides a fairly detailed set of standards to describe what the trustee should be doing, as well as specific practices to measure whether they are exercising adequate care of the assets. Bank trustees may be more cognizant of management principles through 2012 Office of the Comptroller of the Currency (OCC) guidelines.

Given the well-established fiduciary standard of care, one would think that a policy would always be treated professionally and with great care. However, disturbing statutes are in place in some states, and these should concern grantors and beneficiaries alike: these statutes effectively provide a parachute for some trustees to escape the plane while leaving its passengers on board. Either by statute or trust provision, exculpatory statutes may absolve the trustee of his or her responsibilities to the beneficiaries regarding the outcome and performance of the policy (excluding, of course, any outright fraud or criminal acts). These exculpatory statutes do not hold a trustee responsible for losses sustained to a policy due to policy performance.

While this kind of statute or provision might be a reasonable request coming from a family member or friend acting as trustee, the inclusion of such language for professional trustees is cause for concern. Clients entrust their assets to professionals and pay them for professional trustee services, and the expectation is that these professionals will then take care of the client to the best of their ability. A February 2014 article in *Trusts & Estates* magazine poses an interesting question to attorneys: "How many of our settlors would proceed with their trusts if they really understood that their beneficiaries had no enforceable rights in the event of gross negligence or even reckless misconduct of the trustee, or of any misconduct, incompetence, or negligence of the non-fiduciary advisor, short of outright fraud?"[1]

Even without these "parachutes," two court cases have brought to light the issues that may arise within ILITs. In Cochran v. KeyBank,[2] we learned that a trustee who pursues a prudent process is unlikely to be found negligent even if circumstances lead to a less than optimal outcome for their clients. For various reasons, Mr. Cochran's trustee at KeyBank decided to replace their client's existing policy with a new policy that had a significantly lower death benefit and $107,764 in surrender charges. The trustee did this largely to reduce premium payments and to avoid market volatility. When Mr. Cochran died suddenly, his beneficiaries sued KeyBank for breach of fiduciary duties.

---

1 Alexander A. Bove Jr., "The Death of the Trust," *Trusts & Estates*, Feb. 2014, 52–55.
2 n re Stuart Cochran Irrevocable Trust, 901 N.E.2d 1128 (Indiana Court of Appeals, March 2, 2009).

COCHRAN V. KEYBANK

- 1987: Cochran purchases $4.75M universal life and whole life insurance portfolio
- 1999: stock market races; Cochran's insurance agent replaces existing policies with variable universal life and increases death benefit to $8M
- 2001–2002: Stock market declines, nationwide panic ensues
- 2003: $8M was exchanged for a $2.78M guaranteed universal life policy to age 100
- 2004: Cochran dies unexpectedly at the young age of 53

FRENCH V. WACHOVIA Bank

- 2003: French owns two whole life policies with $5M death benefit and $2.2M cash value
- 2004: Whole life policies and cash value exchanged for $5M guaranteed universal life with $0 premiums, saving trust $620K. However, cash value decreases due to new policy type and sizeable commission
- French's reaction: claims "self-dealing" and that Wachovia, by earning more than $500K in commissions, failed its duty of loyalty by putting its own interest before that of the beneficiaries

KeyBank won the trial because they had a "prudent process" in place. In hindsight, KeyBank ould have potentially averted the lawsuit if they had used a more thorough process of comparing data as they sought to change Mr. Cochran's plan from a VUL to a GUL. Hindsight is always 20/20, right? After 9/11, many investors were terrified of stock markets. We can't forget the human psyche when it comes to financial matters.

In *French v. Wachovia Bank,*[3] the trust documents gave the trustee the discretion to "retain, invest, and reinvest in any property . . . regardless of any risk, lack of diversification, or unproductivity involved . . . to continue as trustee and to deal with any trust hereunder without regards to conflicts of interest." This language allowed the trustee to engage in self-dealing by purchasing new life insurance from the bank's insurance brokerage affiliate. In this case, the case facts seem to have met the goal of the trust by securing no-lapse, guaranteed life insurance with $0 premium. Here, Wachovia had broad discretion to invest trust property without regard to conflicts of interest. Wachovia won the case because there was no evidence that they acted in bad faith.

These two early court cases have favorably impacted the way life insurance policies are managed, especially if they include a bank trustee. I've witnessed banks—national and community alike—taking prudent policy management much more seriously by strengthening their

---

3 French v. Wachovia Bank, N.A., 2011 U.S. Dist. LEXIS 72808 (E.D. Wisconsin 2011).

internal support systems. The majority of banks and trust departments now take advantage of third-party review firms (such as my firm, LifeTrust3D™, among others), which is recommended in Section 9 of the Uniform Prudent Investor Act.

∗ ∗ ∗

Consider the following possible scenarios in which a trustee could conceivably be viewed as negligent if his or her actions adversely affected the policy:

- A trustee pays the premium late or early, either of which might result in a higher required premium or loss of policy guarantees.

- A trustee fails to change investment allocations and leaves money in the money market account, even though the policy requires an earnings rate approaching 8 percent to sustain itself.

- A trustee initiates a policy distribution prior to maturity of an earnings segment, causing forfeiture of five years of index policy gains.

- A trustee deactivates the dollar cost averaging feature, allocates investment sub-accounts to prohibited funds or fails to elect the correct portfolio rebalancing option, all of which (in certain situations), may result in permanent termination of the policy's guaranteed death benefit provisions.

- A trustee isn't aware of a looming policy lapse because of failure to secure periodic reprojections of policy performance.
- A trustee fails to recognize upcoming deadlines in the policy death benefit and/or significant premium increases because of reliance upon abbreviated policy information provided by the carrier.
- A trustee fails to pay the additional "term shortfall."

Given these possible pitfalls and the adverse effect that any one of these scenarios might have—combined with the possibility that no one is in the pilot's seat in the first place—gone are the days of assuming a trust-owned life insurance contract can go unmanaged. Grantors, be certain to read and understand trust language in your document, or simply be sure to ask trustees if they are taking proactive steps in managing and monitoring your policy. If not, consider requiring the trustee to engage with a proactive life insurance advisor (who is not about to retire) or a fee-based, independent third-party review firm, which may be appropriate for larger insurance portfolios. Yes, the additional policy service might come at a slightly higher fee—but trust me, you want someone you can *trust* flying your plane and navigating around any dangers that lie ahead. As with any business, you get what you pay for. Trustee fees are on the rise, and for good reason.

ILITs with a nonprofessional trustee are most at risk. Why? Oftentimes, Crummey notices aren't executed and stored properly (or at all), or an annual statement is mistaken for a policy review and policy performance is left to happenstance. Typically, nonprofessional trustees are close friends or family members, and family can sometimes not be so forgiving if mistakes are made with potential inheritances.

Grantors, be certain to read and understand trust language in your document, or simply be sure to ask your trustee if they are taking proactive steps in managing and monitoring your policy. If not, you should look to a proactive life insurance advisor whom you do have confidence in. You might also prefer to seek out a trustee who has a prudent policy management system.

Don't get me wrong—I have seen some ILITs with nonprofessional trustees work quite well, but it's only been that way for the most astute, detailed-oriented, and organized parties. Understandably, grantors may not want to pay fees they consider too high for a professional trustee, or they may not want to answer to a corporate trustee.

All too frequently, though, we have witnessed scenarios where if a professional advisor isn't involved on an annual basis—or if an attorney hasn't trained trustees properly in relation to their duties—paying or not paying fees simply won't matter in the long run. If the IRS finds upon audit that the ILIT hasn't been administered properly, life insurance proceeds may be "clawed-back" and become includable in the grantor's taxable estate. If you are unsure whether your ILIT is being administered properly, be sure to refresh yourself with the flow chart on page 31 and contact your estate planning attorney.

Does any of this mean that all trustees will abandon their duties? Certainly not. In fact, ILIT trustees are much more engaged in 2019 than even in 2015 when I released my first edition of . . . *the Best Policy*. Trustees are taking their fiduciary responsibilities seriously when it comes to trust-owned life insurance. During their audits, bank examiners encourage trust officers of bank trust departments to have a prudent process for ILIT monitoring, just as they do their other unique assets. The word is out: Making sure a pilot is in the pilot's seat gives all parties to the trust the best chance of a successful outcome.

Securing a Pilot and a Flight Plan

As noted, we simply can't make the assumption that someone is looking out for what might happen to an ILIT down the road or taking the necessary steps to give the policy the best possible chance of achieving the desired outcome. What, then, can we do to make sure the policy is being regularly monitored and managed over time?

STEP 1: *Creating a Flight Plan*

For an ILIT, a flight plan takes the form of a life insurance policy management statement. Like an investment policy statement (IPS), the policy management statement defines the necessary policy monitoring guidelines—the guardrails needed to keep the policy on track. It is necessary to understand the environment and constraints under which policy-related decisions should be made. Why was the policy established? Are there targeted policy earnings levels required to sustain said policy? Is there a reason for a concentrated carrier position, rather than a portfolio of policies from multiple carriers? Are there limits on grantor contributions for premium payments? Are there any events or developments that should trigger specific actions, including consideration of alternative policies? Has the need for the policy or the grantor's desire to fund premium gifts changed (a common situation with today's higher estate tax exemption amounts)?

A tangible, written policy management statement with defined monitoring guidelines can document these considerations, as well as many others that can then be used to manage the ILIT. Consider incorporating trust language related to the use of the policy management statement (including provisions for periodic revision of standards as necessary). With such a document, all involved parties will be better informed and held accountable from the beginning. The written policy management statement also lays a foundation upon which to judge any proposed new or replacement policies.

STEP 2: *Ensure Ongoing Policy Management and Monitoring*
While it's impractical for every individual trust to have a specialized policy service system or process, it's *not* impractical for a grantor to insist that any policies be managed by a party employing such a system. A robust policy management process

or software system can provide functionality such as basic policy reporting, premium reminders, status checks, measurement against standards established in the management statement, carrier financial reporting, and even document storage capabilities. While this step may incur a fee, too many things can go wrong in the future with policies that rely solely on ad hoc reporting. When purchasing new coverage, consider only agents who employ (and

> A robust policy management process or software system can provide functionality such as basic policy reporting, premium reminders, status checks, measurement against standards established in the management statement, carrier financial reporting, and even document storage capabilities.

can demonstrate consistently) a system or process with such capabilities. Consider incorporating language into the trust document that requires the trustee to employ such a system, whether internally or via outsourcing to a qualified third party. (It would also be prudent to employ such a system for policies that are not trust-owned.)

STEP 3: *Get a Written Agreement with a Competent Flight Crew*

Discuss the obligations and responsibilities of the trustee with your legal counsel. If you're uncomfortable with the language, look for a trustee willing to provide appropriate services without shirking fiduciary responsibilities. The peace of mind that comes with an experienced pilot flying your plane may make the potential increase in administrative fees or a change in trust situs seem quite reasonable. Relying on annual statements as a life insurance management tool is insufficient. Policy statements are just snapshots of a point in time, and they usually don't accurately project the expected performance of the policy. Include language in your management statement requiring periodic (annual, biannual, or triannual) in-force illustrations to be obtained. However, make sure that the data can be properly interpreted and acted upon. If you haven't been trained to read an EKG correctly, merely having a printed EKG does little to help you make a diagnosis. You need a trusted advisor, someone capable of interpreting the results, identifying any potential problems, collaborating with your other advisors while skillfully directing any necessary plan of action.

Reporting is most useful in conjunction with consultation. Make sure that consultation is with a qualified third party who can provide interpretation and advice related to the information, and who can act efficiently on any required modifications. What if you need an explanation or discussion with trust beneficiaries or grantors? Who is willing and able to handle such a task? Many third-party reporting solutions fail to provide the crucial element of interpretation and consultation, stopping at report generation alone.

It is equally important that any policy management or monitoring services include some level of "fulfillment" services. Analyzing, planning, and adapting are important to the long-term success of a life insurance plan, but any changes have to be implemented properly. Is the agent still around? Is the agent willing to assist? (Remember, the agent may not have a contractual obligation to service the policy—although the good ones do take this seriously.) What if modifications require careful timing and coordination due to policy loans or legal considerations? Who's managing the implementation? Consideration should be given to the ability of policy managers to coordinate the implementation of any requisite modifications. "Reporting only" service providers may leave trustees flying solo when it comes to making changes.

Ideally, an agent is willing to commit—in writing—to providing a given level of policy service, and can provide the policy management system, necessary reporting, interpretation, consultation, and implementation. A simple policy service contract can outline the services the agent is willing to provide. An annual fee may be associated with the management activities, but it's money well spent to give the ILIT the best possibility of producing your desired outcome.

In the absence of a written policy management contract with the writing agent, many trust companies and other professional trustees are now delegating some duties to third-party, fee-based policy management and monitoring firms. Generally, this has resulted in higher trustee fees. ILIT fees have increased to $1,000 annually on the low-end to $3,000 annually on the high-end. These are about double what they were just five years ago, when I released the first edition of by book. Section 9 of the UPIA specifically addresses delegation of investment and management functions. Under Section 9, the trustee may reduce risk while providing a best-practices approach to the management and monitoring of ILIT policies.

Section 9 of the UPIA specifically addresses delegation of investment and management functions. Under Section 9, the trustee may reduce risk while providing a best-practices approach to the management and monitoring of ILIT policies.

Recognizing that the traditional life insurance policy service system is inherently flawed—and frankly, may not exist for 70 percent of insureds—implementing a prudent process today may help mitigate the challenges during flight. The steps suggested in this chapter can provide additional assurance to grantors, beneficiaries, and trustees that the flight has the best chance of reaching the intended destination—while minimizing turbulence as much as possible.

5

An Evolving Landscape: Making Sense of Change

HERE'S A STATISTIC that keeps me up at night: **70 percent of life insurance policies in this country are left orphaned by the original agent and unmonitored.**

Almost three quarters of Americans don't know how their life insurance policies are performing. I think I know why this is: Most people do not object to owning life insurance … they just don't like to pay for it or talk about it. I often joke during my presentations that if I want to ensure a quiet plane ride, early in

> Almost three quarters of Americans don't know how their life insurance policies are performing. I think I know why this is: Most people do not object to owning life insurance … they just don't like to pay for it or talk about it.

the flight I tell the person sitting next to me that I monitor trust-owned life insurance policies for a living. They look at me like I'm crazy, I smile, then they put their ear buds back in. Mission accomplished!

Most people secure a life insurance policy and then stick it in a drawer (literally and metaphorically) until life requires them to look at it. It's understandable, but it's dangerous. We need to know if a policy is meeting its performance expectations and if it's on track. Without a thorough review, people can wake up one day and realize they are at serious risk of losing their policy. Sure, insurance companies mail statements, but statements alone do not even begin to constitute a thorough policy review.

Lawrence S. Rybka, an icon in our industry and a man ahead of his time, explained in 1989 how reputable insurance carriers were illustrating their products at a higher rate of return than was able to be met in prior years.[4] Providing clients illustrations and projections with aggressive assumptions may lead to the sale in the short term, but in the end it will lead to a disappointed client and a failing policy. When a life insurance policy is constructed with aggressive and unrealistic assumptions, it sets the policyholder up to fail. Decreases, even slight ones, in earning rates changes or in the client's premium

---

4 Lawrence S. Rybka, "The Ledger Lie," *Best's Review*, vol. 90, no. 4, August 1989, http://www.valmarkfg.com/site/wp-content/uploads/10X_The_Ledger_Lie.pdf

funding may mean that a client's life insurance plan could be inadequate and in jeopardy of lapse before a death benefit is paid. Policyowners are still relying on sales information and out-of-date illustrations provided to them years ago by the agent that are irrelevant in today's economic environment. That's what keeps me up at night: the idea that all these people could be in trouble and not know it. Life insurance plans were designed to deliver a promise at a single, unknown point in the future. Variance from the original plan (by the carrier or the client) can derail the plan with little warning. My calling is to help prospective and current policyholders make life insurance decisions that are built to stand the test of time.

So why are policies underfunded or underperforming? Let's first consider the history of dividend scales and the impact of a sustained low-interest-rate environment.

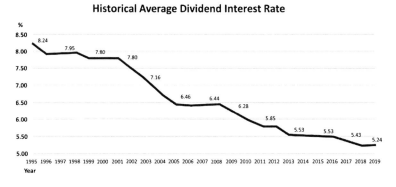

A whole life policy sold in, say, 2000 was anticipating a dividend crediting rate of over 8 percent. Today, dividend crediting rates range from 4–6 percent. Even the strongest of insurance carriers have not had an answer for the low interest rate. Policyholders simply aren't able to "catch-up" from less-than-anticipated dividend rates without re-calibrating their policy (either through increased premium outlay or decreased death benefit).

The life insurance industry has slowly evolved from captive agents selling "one-size-fits-all" policies from a single company. In the early 1980s there were fewer types of policies than there are today, and they were less complex, which made the purchasing process much simpler. These policies were designed around assumptions that may have been reasonable in the double-digit interest rate environment of the time—they even made sense when the stock market roared in the 1990s—but in a time of sustained low-interest-rate and stock market volatility, these simpler plans require substantive adjustments. For example, Whole Life and Universal Life policies dating from that era needed a high interest rate environment to thrive.

The early- to mid-2000s were marked by "no-lapse guarantee" policy types. This essentially means that if a policy is funded on time and every year, it is guaranteed not to lapse. These no-lapse or guaranteed universal life (GUL) policies dominated the marketplace—especially in scenarios in which people wanted to maximize the death benefit in ILITs while minimizing premium outlay. It was an interesting time in the life insurance world—a time when the carrier with least expensive premium generally would get the business.

Carriers are now thinking, "Careful what you wish for, as it just may happen." Carriers underpriced these GUL products and actuaries made incorrect assumptions about interest rates and lapse ratios (the number of policies that would be sold that the client would eventually allow to lapse). GUL seemed to be the perfect policy for trustees managing ILITs. Little did people know that GUL would eventually create its own set of issues for both insurance carriers and policyholders.

Below is a timeline of the industry's evolution:

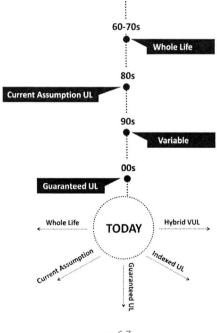

The inability to make changes to premiums or accumulate any meaningful cash value on the policy left consumers with very few options in years when they might have needed to skip premium payments or modify their plans.

Under-reserving for GUL (along with other products with long-term guarantees such as long-term care insurance and annuities) drove prominent insurance carriers to change their business practices drastically. Prominent insurance carriers have since had to exit the life insurance marketplace or sell to private equity firms, leaving policyholders wondering who's in their pilot's seat. Other carriers have increased the pricing on their in-force policyholders in order to shore up their losses.

Products with no-lapse guarantees still exist in today's marketplace, but they are offered by fewer carriers and are generally no longer the low-cost option they once were. Many are now offering secondary guarantees, but only to average life expectancy (generally ages 85–92) vs. a lifetime guarantee (age 120). Product types have changed drastically over the last decade, leading to more choice . . . and more complex products.

The Importance of Ongoing Policy Monitoring

Proactive policy monitoring and management embraces the idea that *change is constant.* A well-managed policy doesn't necessarily mean the policy performs exactly as it was predicted to when sold. Instead, it means when the policy gets off course (as it most likely will), minor adjustments are made to avoid what could amount to a much larger issue down the road.

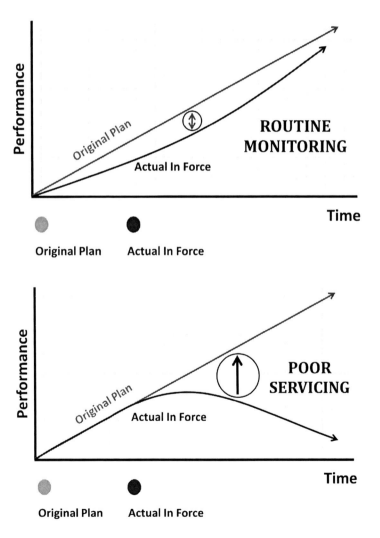

Changes made by the insurance carrier in nonguaranteed elements—such as the dividend, the interest-crediting rate, the cost of insurance, and more—contribute to a policy not behaving as initially predicted. In the low-interest-rate environment that continues to persist, product designs particularly at risk are whole life policies with significant term riders and universal life policies purchased in the 1980s and 1990s. The following chart graphically represents how a whole life and term blend policy may have been sold to clients when interest rates were higher than they are today.

ORIGINAL ILLUSTRATED MECHANICS

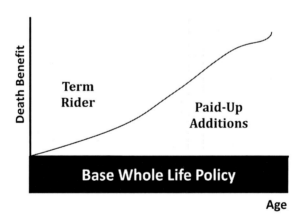

The idea was that a blended policy of Whole Life and Term insurance would simultaneously generate a high enough dividend (Whole Life) and paid-up insurance (Term) to reduce the term component over time while purchasing paid-up additional whole life insurance. As interest rates declined, larger-than-anticipated term riders remained on policies and were a more significant portion of the policy than originally projected. While term insurance is inexpensive for younger insureds, it becomes cost-prohibitive in later years. As a result, many policy owners discovered they owed higher-than-anticipated premiums or had to pay premiums longer than desired to make up for the decline in dividends. Failure to do so might result in a term rider dropping from the policy or the additional premium being paid by an automatic loan. In some cases the term rider may be over half of the total death benefit. The premium loan would have an interest rate as high as 8 percent. These are things we do not want our clients to experience!

MECHANICS WITH DIVIDEND DECLINES

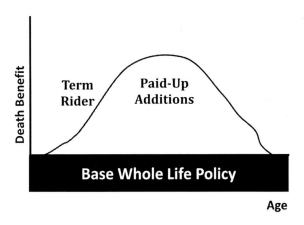

MECHANICS WITH DIVIDEND DECLINES

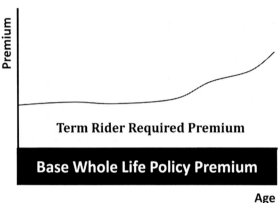

Monitoring policies won't enable us to eliminate problematic policy design, but we can stop simply kicking the can down the road and hoping these issues will self-correct. If we catch these issues early enough, we can help by providing proactive alternatives to get the plan back on track. We can't know for certain what economic, political, or personal factors might impact a client's insurance portfolio in the future. By proactively monitoring policies and adapting to a change, we stand the best chance of protecting the promise once made to a family.[5]

Gary and Mary

To understand this changing landscape, consider two of my clients: Gary and Mary.

---

5 © Valmark Securities, 2014

A colleague referred Gary, a ninety-year-old client. Convinced that his policy was fine as it was, Gary awoke one morning to a notice informing him that his $1 million policy was going to lapse if he didn't come up with a $100,000 premium! The cash value was roughly $300,000 at that time. Gary had already paid about $400,000 in premiums over fifteen years, and he was sure that he'd already entirely paid for the policy. He thought his policy was "paid up." He stated very clearly to me that he wouldn't give the insurance company "another dime of [his] money!" I knew immediately this was going to be a tough situation.

At Gary's age, the options were limited, and since he was still in great health, whatever plan we made couldn't be shortsighted. He wanted to surrender the policy for the $300,000 cash value. However, by working with his insurance carrier, we were able to secure a contractually paid-up death benefit of $580,000. This allowed us to capture the maximum possible paid-up death benefit for Gary, and provided $280,000 more than if he had surrendered the policy. It wasn't the $1 million he had originally planned on, but it was much better than the alternative of a completely lapsed policy with no benefit at all. Sometimes we just have to make the best of a situation. At age ninety, the goal is to maintain the maximum possible benefit for the family. Sometimes the maximum benefit comes in the form of a reduced death benefit, life settlement, or policy surrender.

Unfortunately, Gary's situation is not unique. I dealt with a similar scenario for Mary, a vibrant eighty-five-year-old in excellent health. Mary had two $1 million life insurance policies, one of which was due to mature when she reached age ninety-five. In this case, "mature" meant the cash value at that time would be paid out to the beneficiaries.

Maturity provisions are one of the least understood aspects of older contracts. They essentially render a policy moot when the insured turns a certain age—eliminating the death benefit and simply paying out the policy's cash value. (More on that in a minute.)

The cash value of Mary's particular $1 million policy was projected to be $30,000 at age ninety-five—but now, at eighty-five, the cash value was still a substantial $325,000. Cash value may not always be a top priority for clients focused on maximizing death benefits, but in this case it gave us option. Like I always say, it's better to have cash value and options than no cash value and limited options.

After taking a closer look at Mary's situation, I saw that her second $1 million policy thankfully did *not* have a maturity age of ninety-five. With appropriate funding, it could stay in-force to age 110. However, if it was left underfunded, as was the case, it would lapse when she turned ninety-five. I wanted to figure out a way to help Mary maintain this policy so that it would last for her life-time, even if it meant sacrificing her other policy to do so.

We completed an informal health assessment on Mary to determine whether a life settlement was an option with either policy. (For more on life settlements, see chapter 9.) When it was clear that Mary maintained excellent health and could easily surpass age ninety-five, no life settlement provider wanted to take on the risk to purchase either of her policies. With that information in hand, the trustee—Mary's daughter—made a tough decision on behalf of the beneficiaries. She surrendered the first policy while its cash value was still $300,000, so she could use the proceeds to fund the second $1,000,000 policy.

It is important to note that it took five months to explore all options and receive input from the CPA, investment advisor, trust officer, and beneficiaries. Due to her age, cash values were reducing by an average of $5,000 every month that passed, or $25,000 over the time it took to complete the project. We then deployed the $300,000 to make sure Mary's second policy was well-funded, and now, instead of lapsing at age ninety-five, that $1 million policy would stay in force until Mary reached the age of 110.

> Time always seems
> to work against you
> when you're faced
> with difficult life
> insurance decisions.
> With proactive
> policy monitoring,
> difficult decisions
> can be handled early,
> allowing more time
> for the best possible
> outcome.

At first glance, one might argue that surrendering a $1 million life insurance policy on an eighty-five-year-old's life was poor planning. If Mary were to die suddenly, the decisions made would surely be questioned. However, once we'd documented the file appropriately and collaborated with the family and their advisors, we agreed that sacrificing one policy to save another was best in that situation. If Mary lived past ninety-five, the policies that she'd been funding for years would have suddenly meant nothing. By making an informed and educated decision, we were able to breathe life back into the $1,000,000 policy we felt had the best chance to deliver life insurance proceeds for her family.

In both Gary and Mary's cases, a timely review of their policies would have resulted in a more favorable outcome for their families. I am hopeful that with more trustees proactively pursuing policy reviews, fewer and fewer clients will have to face the challenges that Gary and Mary faced.

With people now living longer, many trust officers will find themselves with clients like Gary and Mary. I tell our trust clients all the time that our top priority is to support trustees (often bank trust departments), so they have the necessary information to advocate for the families they serve. We help facilitate necessary conversations, explore all possible options, and ensure that the trustee and family can make the *best* decision given the family's specific goals and financial situation. Sometimes this means sacrificing one policy to save another.

When policies are monitored routinely, trustees have meaningful communication with their clients. At Life-Trust3D™ we help trustees work more proactively so they don't have to be reactive, as in Gary and Mary's cases. Proactive policy monitoring leads to informed decision-making and better outcomes for beneficiaries, which in turn lead to stronger trustee/client relationships. I want all trustees to remember that life insurance policies were established not just to pay estate taxes, but because someone cared enough to provide for future generations using a dynamic planning tool. Just like the Chinese bamboo tree, routinely watering and nourishing the seeds and soil gives the plant the best chance of success.

In response to these issues—and to hold carriers, agents, and brokers to a higher standard—significant changes are on the horizon to protect policyholders:

1. Regulation 187: Requires agents and insurance companies to document that all life insurance recommendations are both suitable for the client and in the client's best interest. Reg. 187 goes into effect February 1, 2020.

2. Regulation Best Interest (Reg BI): Will require broker-dealers to reduce, disclose, and minimize conflicts of interest. It will require both broker-dealers and registered investment advisors to provide a plain-English Customer Relationship Summary (CRS). Reg. BI, which goes into effect June 2020, will require Certified Financial Planners®, to meet a fiduciary standard for all recommendations of life insurance and annuity products.

3. The NAIC (National Association of Insurance Commissioners) instituted new principle-based reserve requirements beginning January 1, 2020. Life insurance carriers will have to significantly change how they estimate reserves for most types of life insurance contracts. As I complete this second edition of *...the Best*

Policy, carriers are scrambling to re-price their products to comply with new rules designed to better align the new reserve requirements with the features, benefits, and pricing of the life insurance products being offered.

These changes are only the beginning. The life insurance industry is constantly evolving. I recall the words of my eighth-grade teacher, a former Navy SEAL: "Adjust, adapt and overcome." Those of us who are ready for such change are positioned to take care of policyholders well into the future.

Fortunately, it's possible for consumers to recalibrate existing policies or reengineer their underperforming or not-quite-right policies to take advantage of innovations in today's life insurance marketplace. With smart advising and proper monitoring, consumers can make the necessary adjustments so their policy is specifically tailored to their current planning goals.

The last decade has been characterized by increased product choice as a result of the demand for a consumer-centric purchasing environment. It has also resulted in more complex products then ever before. That's why on-going policy monitoring isn't just for older policies.

6

Insurance Review with a Purpose: Asking the Right Questions

JANET, A SWEET, vibrant lady in her seventies, marched into her trust officer's office in frustration. She was recently divorced, in great health, and lived an active lifestyle in her house down by the beach. However, because of her divorce, the assets that she had been living on were still substantial, but not at the level they once were. Her trust-owned life insurance policies had been previously set up so that she was making a gift of $60,000 to the trust each year. The $5 million death benefit was intended to provide for her two adult children and her five grandchildren.

Janet loved her children and their families very much, but over time, the annual $60,000 contribution had become burdensome for her. Her recent divorce put an even bigger stress on her ability to contribute. She'd always been very wealthy, and had been particularly well-off when she purchased her policy twenty years earlier. At the time, a $60,000 annual premium gift was realistic. The trust officer explained to me that she was living off of rent she collected from her commercial real estate properties. As much as she didn't want to admit it, the substantial premium gift was impacting her standard of living. He explained to her that she shouldn't have her standard of living impacted by trying to make her children better off. Just as she would on an airplane, Janet should place her metaphorical oxygen mask on herself first before helping those beside her.

As the trust officer told me Janet's story, I was shocked that no one had stopped to ask her—*since 1998*—whether the $60,000 premium suited her changing lifestyle. The insurance company was strong and reliable, and the trust-owned policy was performing very well, but *no one* had ever asked her if the annual gift was still feasible. As the grantor of the trust, she didn't receive correspondence from the insurance carrier and didn't quite understand how the trust or policies worked. Janet was reluctant to bring the topic up with her other advisors, as the thought of life insurance made her uncomfortable.

One simple question: *Janet, how does it feel to make the $60,000 annual premium gift?* changed the course of the trust and Janet's life. It forged a closer relationship between the trust officer and Janet. Her irrevocable trust had accumulated over $1.8 million in combined cash value between the two policies. The trust officer engaged my company, LifeTrust3D™, to complete our trademarked 3D Process™. By instituting a prudent and independent process and proactively monitoring Janet's policy, the trustee was able to have a conversation with her that hadn't taken place in over twenty years.

Once he understood Janet's fears, the trust officer requested a Design Maximizer Report™ from LifeTrust3D™ to better understand potential alternatives. We produced our report for the trustee—detailing the steps necessary to enhance the delivery value of the insurance program significantly through a tax-free 1035 exchange. This alternative proved to be the solution the trustee was hoping for to eliminate ongoing premium gifts while securing a death benefit similar to the current amount. Because the process was so smooth and productive, the trustee decided to work with our affiliate partner, Colton Groome Insurance Advisors, Inc., to leverage the accumulated policy cash value in the existing trust-owned policies to secure two new ones. Those new policies better helped both Janet and the trust meet their goals of providing the maximum possible benefit to the trust beneficiaries—her beloved children—without requiring further premium gifts from Janet. We helped the trust eliminate the $60,000 premiums *and* secure a death benefit of $5.2 million instead of the original $5 million. Both new policies had a no-lapse, lifetime guarantee. One was built to maintain cash value and one was designed to maximize the death benefit with lower cash value.

After I delivered the new policies to Janet's trust officer, I caught him out of the corner of my eye doing a "happy dance" down the hallway. By referring her to us, he'd saved one of his best clients $60,000 a year and had become Janet's hero. I have never met Janet personally and probably never will, but if you can get a trust officer to do a happy dance, you know you have done something right! In the year after we helped facilitate her policy exchange, Janet took her family on a first-class trip to Europe. Liberated from the annual contribution to the trust, she can now see her family enjoy her resources during her lifetime as opposed to only when she ascends.

The Best Fit

When helping clients review an existing policy, there are two things all grantors need to know: **_The best policy_ is the one that's right for _you_—and the best policy for you may change over time.**

"Well, how do I know which policy is right for me?" a client might ask. Have your clients take into consideration the following: What are their needs today? If they have an existing policy already in force, how have their needs changed since they first purchased the policy? At my firm, LifeTrust3D™, we use a comprehensive Life Insurance Discovery Questionnaire™ that asks these essential questions and more to help us ascertain a client's true needs.

When effectively monitoring in-force policies, advisors and trustees want to first seek to understand the following aspects: premium, death benefit, time horizon, health, performance, risk/reward, and a carrier's financial strength.

> It's important to have your clients take into consideration the following: What are their needs today? If they have an existing policy already in force, how have their needs changed since they first purchased the policy?

Premium

"Has the grantor's ability or desire to fund premiums changed?"

You may find that the $60,000 premium a client was able to fund in 1998 is no longer reasonable with her current income (as was the case with Janet). Or you might find that the client's income and the estate's value have skyrocketed since the initial purchase of the policy, so there's now a need to increase assets outside of his or her taxable estate. A premium may also need to be raised or lowered depending on the client's health, life expectancy, or family medical history. The current estate tax exemption may leave clients believing they have more than enough insurance for estate planning purposes, so they are seeking decreased premium outlays. Remember, though, that estate law is notoriously fluid and may change drastically with every new administration.

Death Benefit

"Does the death benefit still apply to your situation today?"

Maybe a grantor's estate has grown substantially and he or she can leave more behind. Maybe a client *needs* to leave more assets than previously anticipated, as was the case with my client Charles in chapter 2. Maybe the client has children who became wealthier than expected and don't need the money. Or maybe the client has grown estranged from the family and wants the money to be redirected to a favorite charity instead. When one of my client's relationships with his children soured, he decided to leave his inheritance to a local hospital. This is when collaboration with an estate planning attorney and financial advisor becomes invaluable.

Time Horizon

How long do you need life insurance? Is there a portion you need during your working years or for debt protection and another portion desired to meet long-term estate planning goals?

Clients like Charles—the real estate mogul I profiled in chapter 2—may use multiple life insurance policies to meet different goals. We call this a layered approach. Typically, term insurance is used for obligations that may end at a known point in the future, while permanent insurance (whole life, variable life, universal life) is used to meet lifetime planning goals.

Health

"How's your health?"

If an insured's health has declined since the policy was issued, it may make sense to recalibrate the length of time the policy should stay in force. For example, a policy designed to stay in force to age 121 may now only be prudent to fund to age ninety-five. An eighty-year-old with terminal cancer has a $1 million life insurance policy that is designed to stay in force until age one hundred. He may not need to continue funding the current $20,000 annual premium, given his diagnosis. With careful planning and collaboration, the premiums could potentially be reduced or eliminated and the policy maintained in force until age eighty-five or ninety.

On the other hand, sometimes an insured's health improves. We have seen this with individuals who may at one point have been assessed a higher premium for being overweight, having Crohn's disease, being diabetic, or having a certain form of cancer. If these conditions are treated and well controlled—for example, if the insured is cancer-free for more than five years—there's a possibility of more favorable rates.

Sometimes the carrier will allow insureds to improve their underwriting classification with the current policy. In other instances, it may be more beneficial to evaluate a 1035 exchange. IRS Code 1035 allows an insured to purchase a new policy using proceeds from an existing policy on a like-for-like 1035 exchange. By adhering to the 1035 code, one can secure a new policy that may be more favorable without incurring a tax penalty on any gains in the old policy. This is a technique that in select situations we've employed to help clients realign their goals for life insurance and maximize benefits for the trust beneficiaries while adhering to the grantor's funding desires.

Performance

"How long is the policy projected to stay in force based on reasonable earning assumptions and current premium

funding? Does the policy have a contractual premium and death benefit guarantee?

In the 1990s, mutual life insurance carriers boasted dividends of 8 percent or more. In today's sustained, low-interest-rate environment, dividends are closer to 5 percent. That means many policies issued in the 1990s are underperforming and underdelivering on their desired growth. Like gas in your car, life insurance needs fuel in the form of premium dollars, and in older policies, cash value fuels the engines. In a sustained, low-interest-rate environment, policyholders are often funding greater premiums or funding for a longer time horizon than originally projected. In some cases, they have to do both.

Remember how I told you that 70 percent of life insurance policies in the US are left unmanaged and orphaned? Policy performance is an area that if caught early enough, has greater and more palatable solutions. When poor policy performance is sustained for a long period of time, it digs a hole that is difficult and sometimes cost-prohibitive to climb out of. Most insurance carrier annual statements alone are not enough for the layperson to truly understand the inner workings of how their policy is performing relative to the original intention. Without an actual in-force illustration (which has to be specifically requested), policyholders will go along paying the originally planned annual premium thinking everything is fine, until one day they receive a notification of a premium increase. Carriers wait until the increase actually occurs to notify policyholders. They are not structured to inform policyholders in advance of what could be looming in the future.

If you catch underperforming policies early enough, more attractive options are available to remedy the situation. Many times a slight increase in a premium today or a decrease in a death benefit can have a compounding and significant future impact on the policy. It is much better to know about what could be coming and plan for it today than to wait for underperformance to rear its ugly head. Waiting too long can be catastrophic for families.

Risk versus Reward
"How much risk are you willing to take on?"

Every policy type has risks and rewards, advantages and disadvantages. It is crucial that these factors reflect a client's risk tolerance. There's risk in having all of a client's cash value rely solely on general account products (such as universal or whole life policies). There's also risk in relying too heavily on the performance of the investment subaccounts within a separate account (variable policies).

Clients might have a policy with strong contractual guarantees and low premiums, but chances are that they'll be giving up future flexibility gained through cash value accumulation in exchange for those low premiums. It is important to clarify what such policies might mean for clients in the future, and whether they are okay with those repercussions.

Remember, the ultimate goal is to find the *best policy* for a client. The best policy is the policy that matches the client's goals for life insurance. Typically, in ILITs the focus is on efficiently priced death benefit with contractual guarantees. In a typical ILIT, the key is to find the best combination of cost-effective premiums, the most financially stable carrier, the *best* secondary death benefit guarantee (for ILITs, I generally recommend guarantees to at least life expectancy), the *best* potential for future flexibility (provided by cash value), and most importantly, the *best* ongoing commitment for policy management and

> The key is to find the best combination of cost-effective premiums, the best financially stable carrier, the best secondary death benefit guarantee, the best potential for future flexibility, and most importantly, the best ongoing commitment for policy management and monitoring.

monitoring. Remember, ILITs are dynamic, not static . . . and the only thing that is certain in life is change!

Carrier Financial Strength

How do rating agencies report the carrier's performance compared to its peer group? Since I first released my book in 2014, this may be the single biggest change in the industry. Carriers we once thought of as strongholds in the life insurance industry have simply vanished. Carriers such as Phoenix, MetLife/Brighthouse, ING/VOYA, Genworth, SunLife, and Hartford have either been purchased by private equity groups or ceased retail life insurance sales in the US. Many cite the sustained, low-interest-rate environment combined with other factors as the culprits. Policyholders with these carriers must beware and we must help them understand this changing landscape.

* * *

Guy and Claire

The policy review questions in the preceding sections remind me of my favorite case story ever. At the beginning of 2011, as he approached age sixty-five, my client Guy began to see a need to provide more for his family during his lifetime. Guy and his wife, Claire, had three adult daughters whom they loved dearly. Two of their daughters had special-needs children, and the third was struggling to start a small business. They each needed their parents' help.

Guy and Claire were already grantors of an irrevocable life trust, but it was a second-to-die policy, meaning that their daughters wouldn't receive any benefits until both parents had passed away.

The insurance company (one of the fallen giants I mentioned previously) was not as financially stable as it once had been, and Guy began to worry that the company wouldn't be able to make good on its original promise. In 2011, the cash value of their policy was $950,000. The policy itself, which had a death benefit of $5 million, was relatively outdated, and it needed an additional premium to perform as Gary had hoped it would. His other assets weren't liquid at the time, as he was invested heavily in commercial real estate. Guy wanted to know how he could adequately fund his policy while still supporting his family.

In reengineering his policy, Guy wanted to maintain the current death benefit and premium outlay but secure coverage with a more stable carrier. He had been making an annual gift to the trust of $15,000, which worked quite well for him. He also wanted the trust to maintain a $5 million life insurance value for the benefit of his daughters.

We faced two hurdles with Guy and Claire. First, they wanted to engineer a lifetime distribution from the trust to their daughters. Ensuring this kind of payout is not an easy task, and we had to work hard with the trust beneficiaries and the corporate ILIT trustee to approve the distribution. After submitting proof to the trustee that his daughters needed financial assistance to support their families, we were able to receive distribution during Guy's lifetime— a rare occurrence. The trustee's duty is to provide the maximum possible benefit for the trust beneficiaries, and it gets more and more difficult to achieve that goal if money is taken out of the trust during the grantor's lifetime. This type of distribution can only occur if the proper HEMS (Health, Education, Maintenance, and Support) language is contained within the trust document. Guy's daughters needed financial assistance for those very things, so the distribution was granted.

> **The Trustee's duty is to provide the maximum possible benefit for the trust beneficiaries.**

Second, with careful design and consideration of tax consequences, we were able to take a $300,000 loan from the existing policy prior to the policy exchange. In survivorship life insurance—second-to-die policies—the pricing typically depends on the wife's health and age (because we all know women live longer than men!). The new carrier underwrote Claire more favorably than the previous carrier had. This created the pricing arbitrage we needed to make the numbers work. Working closely with the trustee, we were able to exchange policies while carrying over the $300,000 loan to the new policy. We secured a $4.5 million death benefit with Guy's desired annual gift of $15,000.

It's not the mechanics of the policy exchange that make this my favorite story, though. On Christmas Eve of 2011, the trustee deposited $100,000 into the personal bank account of each of the beneficiaries (Guy and Claire's three grown daughters). On December 26, I received a personal phone call from each of them thanking me. By taking the time to reengineer the policy entirely, the trustee and our firm collaborated to make a world of difference to the trust beneficiaries. Now, Guy and Claire can see their daughters enjoy some of the benefits of their many years of work. They still have life insurance, but their daughter's lives are better today because of our efforts.

As trustees and advisors considering how to make each policy more purposeful, never forget to ask *why*. Why was this policy purchased and why is it needed today? The answers to these questions will put you on the path to creating *the best policy* for your clients. And, if you're lucky, it'll help you remember why you are in this business in the first place.

7

Insurance Maintenance with a Purpose: How Can Fiduciaries Effectively Monitor Policies?

AT MY FIRM, LifeTrust3D™, our 3D Process™ provides continuous monitoring and review of our clients' dynamic life insurance policies. Our unique process is built specifically to serve and support fiduciaries in meeting two key standards of responsible fiduciary management: the Uniform Prudent Investor Act (UPIA) and the Office of the Comptroller of the Currency (OCC). An effective policy manager needs to understand and comply with these two fiduciary guidelines. Before going further into how our 3D Process™ works, let's look at these fiduciary statutes.

The UPIA

Written by the American Law Institute in the 1990s and adopted by more than forty states, the Uniform Prudent Investor Act (UPIA) requires that trustees acting in their

> In the UPIA, fiduciaries find a code of conduct for advising and management—a guide that not only encourages, but legally requires cultivating a best policy for each client.

fiduciary capacity demonstrate a particular process for selecting, managing, and monitoring all assets held in the trust. In the UPIA, fiduciaries find a code of conduct for advising and management—a guide that not only encourages, but legally requires cultivating a best policy for each client.

The UPIA has five major governing principles:

1. *The standard of prudence is applied to any investment as part of the total portfolio, rather than individual investments . . . "portfolio" embraces all assets.*

2. *The tradeoff in all investing between risk and return is identified as the fiduciary's central consideration.*

3. *All categoric restrictions on types of investments have been abrogated; the trustee can invest in anything that plays an appropriate role in achieving the risk/return objectives of the trust and that meets the other requirements of prudent investing.*

4. *The long-familiar requirement that fiduciaries diversify their investments has been integrated into the definition of prudent investing.*

5. *The much-criticized former rule of trust law forbidding the trustee to delegate investment and management functions has been reversed.*[6]

Prior to the passage of this act, there was no standard ethical code that fiduciaries could use as a guide in making prudent decisions. There are nine sections of the UPIA, each of which provides details to help trustees and fiduciaries uphold those five principles. The UPIA is the standard upon which we built LifeTrust3D™.

Let's take a look at how each section applies to the management of trust-owned life insurance policies.

Section 1: *The Prudent Investor Rule*
First and foremost, the UPIA declares that a trustee who invests and manages assets owes a duty to the beneficiaries. In other words, trustees should treat others as they would want to be treated. Section 1 is the Golden Rule that carries the rest of the Act, and it's the code that all advisors should live by, whether they are involved with life insurance or other facets of the industry.

---

6 Uniform Prudent Investment Act of 1995, Section 9.

SECTION 2: *Standard of Care; Portfolio Strategy; Risk and Return Objectives*

Section 2 requires a trustee to manage trust assets as a prudent investor would. The trustee shall exercise reasonable care, skill, and caution. That sounds reasonable. Decisions should be made by evaluating all assets in the trust, not in isolation, but as part of an overall strategy in which risk and return objectives are reasonably suited to meet the trust's long-term objectives. This requires consideration of not only the client's overall portfolio but also general economic conditions. A good trustee considers the client's overall financial circumstances in light of current economic and political environments.

SECTION 3: *Diversification*

This section advises trustees and advisors to diversify the investments of a trust unless the trustee reasonably determines that, because of special circumstances, the purposes of the trust are better served without diversifying. When it comes to life insurance, we interpret diversification to mean that just like a well-diversified investment portfolio, larger insurance portfolios benefit from diversification among both insurance carrier and policy types.

SECTION 4: *Duties at Inception of Trusteeship*
Within a reasonable time after accepting a trusteeship or receiving assets, a trustee shall review the trust assets, and shall make and implement decisions concerning the retention and disposition of assets in order to bring the trust portfolio into compliance with the purpose of the trust. At Life-Trust3D™, we complete "Pre-Acceptance" reviews of life insurance policies prior to a trustee taking on a new client or policy. This is one of the most important duties we fulfill for our clients, so they do not unknowingly take on an unknown risk.

SECTION 5: *Loyalty*
Duty of loyalty is a topic most often discussed within trust departments. Grantors call in wanting to make changes to trust assets, but it is the beneficiaries who are owed the sole duty of loyalty by the trustee. This is quite the slippery slope for some trustees, as they are often caught between a rock (the grantor) and a hard place (beneficiaries).

Beneficiaries need to feel as though someone's on their side; this section encourages trustees and advisors to remain loyal to the beneficiaries and act in their best interest.

SECTION 6: *Impartiality*

This section takes care of those trusts that have more than one beneficiary; the trustee must make fair decisions that are in the interest of *all* the beneficiaries. This section is important for fiduciaries managing policies for an entire family. It derives from the duty of loyalty in requiring the trustee to respect the interests of all the beneficiaries listed in the Trust document.

SECTION 7: *Investment Costs*

Section 7 requires trustees to mitigate costs, only incurring those that are reasonable and in the best interests of the portfolio and the beneficiaries. Internal charges or "costs" vary among insurance carriers and policy types. It is important for trustees to understand the internal cost structure of the policies they trustee. With certain carriers increasing internal cost of insurance charges, this will continue to be an area of focus for third-party review firms such as LifeTrust3D™.

SECTION 8: *Reviewing Compliance*

Section 8 ensures that compliance with the UPIA is determined by current, not past, economic factors. They say, "Hindsight is always 20/20." The UPIA is not as focused on outcome as it is on having a due diligence process in place. None of us know what tomorrow holds; all we can do is do the best job for clients based on facts and circumstances today.

SECTION 9: *Delegation of Investment and Management*
This section is crucial to ILIT trustees. Delegation to a third party of certain responsibilities, such as the ongoing monitoring of life insurance policies, is now not only accepted; it's common practice among both large national banks and regional and community banks with trust departments.

The UPIA is an excellent guide for monitoring and managing policies because it lays out a prudent and disciplined process that values expertise and prioritization of the client's best interest. It advises fiduciaries to diversify within each portfolio where possible, as any financial advisor would with an investment portfolio. It provides guidance, encouraging fiduciaries to seek out third parties when dealing with unique assets that may be outside their area of expertise.

It's important to note that not all states follow the UPIA. Certain states have exculpatory statutes under which trustees can avoid liability for failed policies. Because there are states in which trustees can avoid liability in their handling of a policy, it is important to always seek out a *trusted* advisor who can make sure policies are handled responsibly. Certain national banks have built entire teams, sometimes comprising as many as ten or even twenty trust officers, whose sole job is to shepherd the policies being trusteed. If you have questions regarding ILITs, seek guidance from your industry peers.

The OCC

The Office of the Comptroller of the Currency is an independent bureau inside the Department of the Treasury. The OCC issues handbooks that help protect all parties involved in fiduciary agreements. The OCC handbook's guidance for "unique and hard-to-value assets" lays out the best practices for ILIT management. The handbook outlines the criteria that a fiduciary should consider in the maintenance of policies:

- **Sufficiency of premiums:** The bank fiduciary must determine whether current premiums are sufficient to maintain the policy to maturity or to meet the insured's life expectancy.
- **Suitability of the insurance policy:** If the bank fiduciary identifies concerns with the condition of the insurance provider or if that provider

does not meet the needs of the grantor or beneficiaries, the policy may need to be replaced.
Tax changes that could affect the suitability of
the policy should be assessed.

- **Carrier selection:** The bank fiduciary needs
to evaluate the carrier's financial condition.
To the extent that insurance carrier ratings
are available, they generally lag corporate and
market events and should be used principally
as indicators of a firm's creditworthiness.

- **Appropriateness of investment strategy:** The
bank fiduciary must evaluate the appropriateness of investments of any segregated account
to support the cash value.[7]

Third-Party Expertise

Both the UPIA and OCC literature on ILIT point out that
a third party can provide valuable expertise outside of a
trustee's knowledge base. At LifeTrust3D™, we developed
our 3D Process™ to offer that level of expertise for trustees.

Additional Insights

It's worth having both the UPIA and OCC handbook
on life insurance bookmarked in a browser. In addition

---

7 Office of the Comptroller of the Currency, *Comptroller's Handbook: Asset
Management, Unique and Hard-to-Value Assets*, 2012, 37–39.

to the standards and recommendations laid out in these documents, I have a few more to offer, as an advisor and educator of trust officers and fiduciaries:

1. **Craft a policy management statement and/ or policy monitoring guidelines** for each ILIT (a flight plan, as described in chapter 3). A policy management statement establishes, clarifies, and solidifies the monitoring criteria you'll follow for that particular trust, just as you might for an investment portfolio. In a policy management statement, you'll determine the parameters for policy lapse age, premium funding, insurance carrier financial strength, crediting rate, and death benefit—all the details that need to be taken into account to create and maintain *the best policy* for your client. If crafting a policy management statement for each policy is overwhelming due to the number of policies being managed, it is widely accepted to have a Corporate Standards of Prudence governing how policies are managed and how important decisions are made. LifeTrust3D™ offers free sample documents on our website: www.lifetrust3d.com/tools. Hint: Password is DiscoverLT3D.

2. **Establish important reminders throughout the year** to help you track trust funding reminders to grantors, premium due dates, Crummey notices, and policy review dates for each trust-owned life insurance policy.

3. **Utilize a technology platform that monitors policies' performance, deadlines, and needs.** Most of them have automated calendar services and reminders to keep you on track. At LifeTrust3D™ we use the industry's leading technology platform, *Proformex*, created by industry innovator and my friend, Mike Pepe.

4. **Create annual policy reviews to share with your client**. Annual policy statements from the insurance company do not provide enough information to understand how the policy is performing. Even if they don't read the annual policy reviews, clients will know their trustee is taking care of them.

5. **Reevaluate all goals of trust-owned policies annually**. This is the perfect time to revisit the reason they took out the policy in the first place and understand what (if anything) has changed in their life.

8

Insurance Design with a Purpose: Matching Your Life Insurance to Your Needs as They Change (and They Will!)

MUCH OF THIS book has been about monitoring life insurance policies in a changing landscape. The purpose of this chapter is to provide trustees, attorneys, accountants, and other professionals with a foundation on which to build a meaningful life insurance conversation. Your clients will need an expert to assist not only with the selection of *the best policy*, but with the monitoring and management of that policy.

In most cases, one of two major factors drives a client's policy decisions: How much life insurance do I need? or how much premium am I willing to fund? Some clients come

> In most cases, one of two major factors drives a client's policy decisions: How much life insurance do I need? or how much premium am I willing to fund?

in with a specific benefit number in mind. For example, they've decided each of their two kids should have $1 million, so they want a $2 million benefit regardless of the premium outlay. Other clients prioritize their ability to contribute a certain amount to the trust annually rather than focus on the death benefit number.

Any true insurance professional would prefer to begin the dialogue somewhere other than price, but it is inevitably the first question, especially as it relates to trust-owned life insurance. The chart below will provide a response to clients, with the expectation that the next question will be, "Well, which one is best for my situation?"

Sample Policy Pricing for $1 Million in Coverage

"Which one is best for me?" is the exact question we want to hear. This is where expert insurance advisors prepare to listen, discern, and apply their knowledge—three of the many ways in which we differentiate ourselves within a highly commoditized industry. The chart below provides a simple breakdown of the advantages and disadvantages of different policy types.

To begin the process of finding the best policy, we give clients a preliminary questionnaire to better understand their goals. This also allows us to document the purpose

The required premiums for life insurance vary by age, risk classification, and product type. Even within a given product type, each carrier has a unique combination of pricing and features that results in wide ranges of potential required premiums. The tables below show approximate ranges for required premiums on various product types and ages.

MALE- PREFERRED NONSMOKER

Product	AGE 45		AGE 55		AGE 65		AGE 75	
	LOW	HIGH	LOW	HIGH	LOW	HIGH	LOW	HIGH
Guaranteed Universal Life (GUL)	$7,300	$14,800	$12,100	$20,700	$21,400	$34,500	$41,400	$54,500
Hybrid Variable Universal Life	$9,000	$13,700	$14,000	$31,100	$24,200	$38,200	$45,300	$67,600
Universal Life (UL)	$7,000	$13,100	$11,300	$20,800	$20,200	$31,400	$39,600	$59,400
Indexed Universal Life (IUL)	$7,000	$11,600	$11,400	$19,900	$20,700	$36,000	$38,800	$67,700
Whole Life	$7,000	$21,900	$21,000	$37,300	$32,300	$70,200	$61,500	$85,000

FEMALE- PREFERRED NONSMOKER

Product	AGE 45		AGE 55		AGE 65		AGE 75	
	LOW	HIGH	LOW	HIGH	LOW	HIGH	LOW	HIGH
Guaranteed Universal Life (GUL)	$5,900	$9,400	$10,200	$20,000	$17,800	$33,100	$34,600	$52,800
Hybrid Variable Universal Life	$7,400	$12,400	$11,300	$20,100	$21,400	$32,700	$39,400	$55,000
Universal Life (UL)	$6,000	$11,500	$9,500	$18,200	$16,800	$27,200	$30,600	$52,300
Indexed Universal Life (IUL)	$6,100	$10,400	$10,100	$17,500	$17,400	$30,800	$33,300	$54,400
Whole Life	$11,500	$18,600	$18,300	$30,800	$28,000	$55,600	$53,000	$73,900

for life insurance through a policy management statement. The policy management statement is like an investment policy statement (IPS) for an investment portfolio; it provides the trustee documentation of why a certain carrier and plan design was selected based on the goals of the trust. Knowing that there is no "one-size-fits-all" insurance plan and that every policy type has advantages and disadvantages, we emphasize five critical factors in the policy selection process. These five selection criteria, along with medical underwriting, will have the most significant impact in answering the client's first question: "How much does life insurance cost?"

Product Type

WHOLE LIFE *Without term riders*

ADVANTAGES	DISADVANTAGES
Guaranteed Premiums – cannot change	Expensive – highest premium for the death benefit
Fully reserved with cash values available to policy owners	Inflexible design – difficult to change premium or death benefit
Over 100+ years' history. Whole life has consistently paid benefits	Actual dividends are unlikely to be as high as currently illustrated dividend crediting rates
	Dividends paid at insurance company's discretion

UNIVERSAL LIFE *Without secondary death benefit guarantees*

ADVANTAGES	DISADVANTAGES
Lower projected premium	Client at risk for having to pay higher premium
A great amount of premium flexibility	Company can change cost of insurance, credited rates and expense changes
Adjustable death benefit	Very little is guaranteed- almost everything is subject to company's discretion

UNIVERSAL LIFE *With secondary death benefit guarantees*

ADVANTAGES	DISADVANTAGES
Low guaranteed premium	Very high expense loads lead to low cash values
Premiums remain flexible. However, changes in premiums or timing of payment may adversely affect guarantees	Inability to adjust charges may create financial pressure on the company
	No potential for better-than-guaranteed results
	Little or no ability to adapt policy to future changes
	If not properly managed, guarantees can be lost, leading to expensive "catch-ups" or policy lapse

VARIABLE UNIVERSAL LIFE *Without secondary death benefit guarantees*

ADVANTAGES	DISADVANTAGES
All expenses are described in prospectus	Client has a higher premium if targeted returns are not achieved as illustrated
Client selects investments	Volatility of returns affects policy performance
Historically higher rates of return can be used to reduce premium payments, increase benefits or provide flexibility	Some clients are not sophisticated enough to understand or manage product
Additional safety of separate accounts gives maximum protection from insurance company insolvency	Product may not be suitable for very conservative policyholders

VARIABLE UNIVERSAL LIFE *With secondary death benefit guarantees*

ADVANTAGES	DISADVANTAGES
All advantages of #3 and #4	These products have charges for the guarantees
Combines flexibility, low overall cost and potential for strong performance	Younger clients with robustly funded VUL policies may prefer lower charges of VUL
	Guaranteed premiums are usually higher with nonvariable universal life
	The upside potential may not offset this for older clients
	Fewer insurance companies offer this product

INDEXED UNIVERSAL LIFE *Without secondary death benefit guarantees*

ADVANTAGES	DISADVANTAGES
All advantages of #2	All disadvantages of #2
Somewhat higher cash value growth potential than Universal Life	Extremely complex product mechanics usually accompanied by various administrative technicalities that may materially alter the product performance results
If chosen indices experience a loss, cash value protected by a minimum floor (usually 0%)	Limited historical information on carrier treatment of nonguaranteed performance elements related to the Index in various economic environments
	It is a product that gives the insurance company the most latitude to change key nonguaranteed elements to the detriment of policyholders

1. **Safety:** the degree of protection afforded to your plan. Safety is measured by the financial strength of the chosen life insurance carrier and by the secondary premium and death benefit guarantees included in the life insurance contract. Guarantees, backed by the claims-paying ability of the insurance carrier, may provide comforting assurance that the premium and/or death benefit is *guaranteed* to average life expectancy, or age one hundred, or for an insured's lifetime. In today's life insurance environment, the longer the guarantee, the higher the premium.

Knowing that there is no "one-size-fits-all" insurance plan and that every policy type has advantages and disadvantages, we emphasize five critical factors in the policy selection process—safety, certainty, flexibility, equity, and premium. These five selection criteria, along with medical underwriting, will have the most significant impact in answering the client's first question: "How much does life insurance cost?"

2. **Certainty:** the degree of confidence one has that the policy design parameters will perform as expected. This may include nonguaranteed factors such as the insurance carrier's dividend rate for whole life policies, the interest-crediting rate on a universal life policy, or the earnings rate assumption on a variable or indexed universal life policy. Every illustration has a disclaimer stating, "This is a life insurance illustration and not a contract. Actual results may vary from the illustrated values shown in in this illustration." The factors the insurance carrier controls and the factors the policy owner controls are all subject to change.

3. **Flexibility:** the ability to modify and adapt a plan to life's surprises. This is a key element. Whether it's a need to change premiums, access cash values, or reduce the protection amount, future flexibility is important.

4. **Equity:** the ability of a policy to build cash value over time. Generally, policies that build cash value may require a greater premium outlay than those that don't, but they often provide more flexibility in the event that the needs or goals of the trust change in the future.

5. **Premium:** Although many decisions are made based on the desired premium outlay, finding a

premium that matches a client's budget, risk tolerance, and desired funding timeline helps tailor the plan to a client's overall goals.

Underwriting

While insurance design is critical, nothing is more important to securing life insurance than the medical underwriting process. Advocacy is critical in negotiating the best possible offers from insurance carriers.

Many consumers believe that you purchase life insurance with premium dollars, but it's more complicated than that. You purchase it first with your health, good character, and financial stability, and *then* with your premium dollars.

Carriers have a way of finding out about the risks they take on when insuring policyholders through databases such as the Medical Information Bureau, motor vehicle reports, prescription searches, and IRS records. To avoid surprises, we recommend trustees work with independent insurance advisors that first begin with informal underwriting *before* making a formal recommendation and submitting a formal application to an insurance carrier. Colton Groome Insurance Advisors uses a private underwriting rating evaluation process (PURE Process™) for insureds looking to secure new life insurance or exchange an older policy for a new policy on the most favorable

Carriers have a way of finding out about the risks they take on when insuring policyholders through databases such as the Medical Information Bureau, motor vehicle reports, prescription searches, and IRS records. To avoid surprises, we recommend trustees work with independent insurance advisors that first begin with informal underwriting before making a formal recommendation and submitting a formal application to an insurance carrier.

terms possible. The PURE Process™ allows underwriters to assess all aspects of the client's insurability *prior* to finalizing any insurance recommendation or completing a formal life insurance application. If there are potential issues with prospective life insurance consumers, we want to find out up front and then navigate the insurance landscape using our decades of expertise.

Why is it important to go through this additional work prior to submitting a formal application? To help clients secure life insurance on the most favorable terms. Advocating for a preferred risk class up front can save multiple thousands of dollars over the client's lifetime (see the graph below).

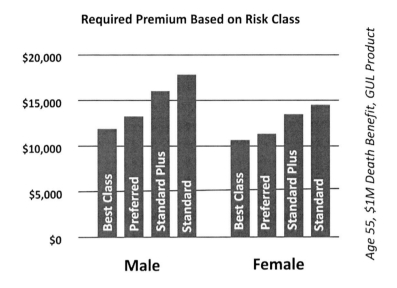

Required Premium Based on Risk Class

Being truly independent allows an insurance advisor the autonomy to sit on the same side of the table as the client. With heightened fiduciary standards and a focus on delivering life insurance solutions in the client's best interest, the bar for excellence has just been raised. To truly succeed, insurance advisors will need to set their self-interest aside and document that they are acting in the best interest of their client. Fortunately, thanks to my father, this is the only way of doing business I've ever known. Having been a captive agent early in his career, he realized in the early 2000s that he wanted to be truly independent. He's always been a man ahead of his time, and always instilled in us our firm's core values:

- Client First
- Integrity Always
- Continuous Pursuit of Excellence
- Teamwork
- Fanatical Attention to Preparation and Execution

These were the seeds my father planted in me, which I have watered and nourished ever since. Remember, the preparation and due diligence we perform on our clients' behalf is like nurturing a Chinese bamboo tree. If we methodically and prudently tend to policies in their infant stage, it will save us from trouble down the road. We get to sit back later and watch the plant grow and multiply.

9

Life Settlements and Maturity Provisions: What You Need to Know

Tate,

Well it looks like you have pushed the sale past the finish line. Thank you and your team for getting this done in a professional and excellent manner. It is very rewarding for me to see my children enjoy some extra money instead of them waiting until I'm gone. I appreciate your service.

THESE ARE THE kinds of notes that really hit home and help me remember what's important—helping families. This one was sent to me by Michael, a client who reached out to me last year with a request. "I'm going to live another fifteen years," he said. "I want to see my kids enjoy the funds I set aside for them while I'm living, as opposed to waiting until I've died. I no longer want to fund $50,000 annual premiums for my life insurance." After working with Michael and reviewing all the options, it was clear that a life settlement was the best option for him.

Life settlements are on the rise. It is important that trust officers understand them, as they may be the best course of action for certain clients.

A life settlement is the sale of an existing life insurance policy on the secondary market to a third party for a sale price that exceeds the policy's cash surrender policy. In other words, an investor group purchases a policy from the policy owner and takes over making premium payments on the plan until the insured person dies. At that point, the investment group collects the death benefit. For reasons I'll explain in a moment, life settlements tend to involve insureds over sixty-five years old with some health impairment. Life settlements used to be considered taboo, but now they are much more accepted for insureds and grantors no longer able or no longer willing to continue making premium gifts.

Why would an insured person want to sell their policy?

Remember, as I've stated throughout this book, the life insurance landscape has changed drastically in the last twenty years. Lower interest rates, increasing cost of insurance charges, and changes in the estate tax laws have left some insureds asking whether they really need as much life insurance today as they did in the past—or if they even need life insurance at all. Even if they want to maintain their life insurance, are they willing to fund the increased premiums many would have to pay in order to fund and sustain policies that have underperformed and now are projected to lapse before the insured dies?

When policy owners receive the dreaded letter from their insurance carrier that premiums are increasing—sometimes more than doubling—they begin evaluating their options. For older insureds, a life settlement may be an alternative to funding higher-than-anticipated premiums. I've outlined some cases of these types of older policy owners in previous chapters: Gary, Mary, and Janet, for example, all struggled to pay premiums greater than what their retirement cash flow could support.

Remember, too, the 2018 Tax Cuts and Jobs Act now allows individuals to exclude over $11 million (indexed for inflation) from their taxable estate ($22 million for a married couple) through the year 2025. This significantly reduces the number of estates subject to estate taxes at this time. Many policies we now see being considered for a life settlement were originally purchased in the early 2000s, when the exemption was between $1 and $3.5 million. Those policy owners feel they no longer need to protect their estates, do not want to pay their premiums anymore, and want their loved ones to benefit today, while they are alive and can see the smiles on their families' faces.

My client Michael owned two $500,000 life insurance policies totaling $1,000,000. He was used to funding a total of $20,000 annually, but after his estate planning attorney referred him to us for a policy review, the premium necessary to sustain $1,000,000 to age 100 increased to $50,000 annually. Surprised by the outcome of the review, he wanted to take some time to reflect on the purpose of his life insurance.

After consulting with his attorney and investment advisor, he knew he could afford the increased premium required to maintain viable policies. However, he came to the conclusion that he preferred to use the $50,000 annually to make lifetime gifts to his children and grandchildren so he could see them enjoy his good fortune. He decided to sell the policies in the life settlement marketplace through Colton Groome Insurance Advisors. In addition to the $50,000 of freed-up annual cash flow, the net sales proceeds from the life settlement totaled $300,000.

Michael took his family on a huge vacation, flying out of state to see his grandkids play football and see the smiles on his family's faces. That's what I call a win! Stories like Michael's, and the relationships we build with our clients, make my work gratifying.

Okay, so now we know why some policy owners want to sell their policies for cash, but why would an investment group want to buy someone's life insurance policy?

Some investor groups, known as life settlement providers, are looking for assets that do not correlate to the stock market. Bluntly, mortality meets that criterion. Life settlement providers understand that the inherent internal rate of return (IRR) within life insurance policies can be favorable in the right set of circumstances. Simply stated, the purchase price + premiums paid is projected to be substantially less at the insured's life expectancy than the life insurance death benefit proceeds. Investment groups seek out policies on people over sixty-five years old with a health impairment. They generally want to purchase policies with a life expectancy of less than twelve years.

To understand how this works, let's consider another recent client of mine: Celeste. She was seventy-eight years old and she owned three $1 million life insurance policies, with a total value of $3 million. She received a letter from the insurance carrier notifying her that her cost of insurance charges (COI) had increased substantially. The COI increase meant Celeste's premium payments had doubled from $100,000 to $200,000 a year. That $100,000 annually was already hard for her to swing, and now they wanted $200,000? Like many older Universal Life policies, Celeste's policies had no meaningful cash value. A policy surrender would have meant that after funding $100K per year for close to fifteen years, she would receive nothing back from the carrier upon a policy surrender. Surely there had to be another option.

Through the life settlement marketplace, we were able to sell two of Celeste's policies for $400,000 each and one of them for $300,000. Celeste and her family—burdened by an exorbitantly high premium and unable to surrender their policies for any meaningful cash value—ended up getting $1.1 million. Although it wasn't quite what she'd paid in over those fifteen years, it was much more than $0. She and her family were grateful for the outcome.

The investor group or life settlement provider that purchased Celeste's policies did the following calculus to determine a purchase price for her policies: They did a full medical work-up on this seventy-eight-year-old woman, and calculated her life expectancy based on her health. They then factored the premium outlay they would need to pay—$200,000 for every year Celeste would live. They concluded that it was worth buying the policies at $1.1 million and paying that yearly premium in order to get a $3 million return on investment. An entire competitive bid process among multiple life settlement providers went on behind the scenes to negotiate an offer as high as $1.1M for these policies.

You can see why these investment groups want to purchase policies with a life expectancy of less than twelve years. They want returns of anywhere from 8 to 12 percent.

Insurance carriers generally do not like life settlements. Think about Celeste for a minute: She paid $100,000 for fifteen years, spending a total of $1,500,000. If she surrenders her policies for a few thousand dollars, the insurance carrier wins. They never have to pay a life insurance claim, and they have received $1,500,000. They count on policies lapsing when they price them. Now, a life settlement provider with deep pockets steps in to purchase a set of policies that would have never resulted in a death claim. How *dare* they!

A secondary market reduces the percentage of cancelled and surrendered policies, known as the "lapse ratio." Traditionally, carrier actuaries price "lapse ratios" into their products. They know that a certain percentage of policyholders will fund premiums for a long time, then cancel or surrender their policies for cash. With the growing life settlement marketplace, their lapse ratios may not be materializing as the actuaries anticipated. Due to this, we are seeing certain insurance carriers now offer "enhanced cash surrender value options" to policyholders, enticing them to surrender some of the most efficiently priced life insurance policies in the marketplace.

Carriers look for ways to protect themselves and their stockholders when they know they've priced certain products too low. This becomes even more evident in a low-interest rate environment. Therefore, they offer to buy back policies that may have a cash surrender value of $150,000 for a premium of, say, $225,000. That way, they get these underpriced policies off their books (kind of like banks do for bad debt) while also taking a $1,000,000 liability off their books (the death benefit of the policy they are buying back).

Generally, if a carrier offers to purchase a policy back from a policyholder, that means it is priced too low. Don't take their bait—hold on to these policies if at all possible!

To be clear, life settlements are generally viewed as a last-resort option when the alternative is to surrender the policy or allow it to lapse due to inability to fund the necessary premium. There are very specific circumstances that warrant the selling of a policy on the secondary market. Ideally, a well-monitored policy would be adjusted to maintain an affordable premium and appropriate death benefit. Nobody wants to surrender a policy for next to nothing. Life settlements can be a last resort that help your clients recoup value on a problematic policy.

What Is a Life Settlement?

A life settlement is the sale of an existing life insurance policy on the secondary market to a third party for a sale price that exceeds the policy's cash surrender value.

- The owner sells the policy in exchange for a lump sum settlement that can be higher than cash surrender value.
- The third-party institutional investor becomes the owner of the policy, makes premium payments, and collects the death benefit at the insured's death.

Maturity Provisions

With a life settlement, you are looking to help a policyholder make the most of a life insurance policy that no longer works for their situation. But what if the policy seems to be in great shape and is in force to "maturity," and then suddenly, at age ninety-five, ninety-eight, or one hundred, the life insurance benefit reverts back to its cash value? The life insurance benefit you thought you had could vanish. That's the kind of contractual provision that makes a trustee wake up in a cold sweat. But it's not a nightmare—it's a maturity provision.

Maturity provisions are *the single most important thing* I work to educate people about when I speak at trust conferences and with our clients.

In the 1980s and 1990s, it was commonplace for insurance carriers to include maturity provisions at age ninety-five, ninety-eight, or one hundred. Policyholders were told that if they outlived these provisions they would "beat" the insurance carrier and get paid a handsome reward for doing so. It was reasoned that the cash value of their policies would be equal to or greater than the original death benefit. Part of the value would be created by the policy owner's premium contributions, but the majority of the value would be created by the insurance carrier's assumed earnings within the policy.

If only reality lined up with theory. As you know, interest rates changed, the cost of insurance increased, and dividends decreased. These provisions were seldom discussed, since after all, who was going to live that long? If they were discussed, many agents would position policy maturity as a reward for outliving your life insurance. It was kind of like finding a pot of gold at the end of the rainbow, so it didn't seem to be an issue on the surface. Then came the perfect storm: increased life expectancies combined with significantly lower-than-projected cash-value accumulation. Today, maturity provisions (with many but not all policies) are not the pot of gold at the end of the rainbow, but the lump of coal with which parents threaten misbehaving children around the Christmas season.

In the 1990s, maturity provisions were highly theoretical. Very few Americans were living into their late nineties. According to the *Wall Street Journal,* in 1980 there were 32,194 centenarians in America. By 2010, there were 53,364 Americans living past age one hundred.[8] Last week, a woman in my home state of North Carolina turned 109. People are living longer. Maturity provisions are a real issue today.

The Furious Case of Mr. Lebbin

If you want to understand the human cost of maturity provisions, consider Gary Lebbin. The first time I heard Mr. Lebbin's story, I literally got sick to my stomach. (It is currently being litigated—see *Lebbin v. Transamerica*, US District Court, Southern District of Florida, Case No. 9:18-cv-80558)

Mr. Lebbin was born in 1917 in Berlin. He fled Nazi Germany in 1938 and ended up penniless Baltimore, Maryland. Mr. Lebbin worked hard and made a name for himself in the paint industry—eventually owning over

---

8 Leslie Scism, "Happy 100th Birthday! There Goes Your Life Insurance," *Wall Street Journal,* July 20, 2017, https://www.wsj.com/articles/happy-100th-birthday-there-goes-your-life-insurance-1500548402

fifty retail paint shops in the Baltimore-Washington area. He married the love of his life and started a family. He is the best of America.

Mr. Lebbin turned one hundred years old in 2017. Shortly before his birthday, he received a letter from his life insurance carrier, Transamerica, notifying him that his life insurance policies (two of them totaling $3.2 million in death benefits) had matured. Instead of his beneficiaries receiving the life insurance benefits at his passing or receiving a sizeable cash value, the contractual maturity provision in Mr. Lebbin's policy stated that the maturity value would be equal to the cash value at age of maturity. This amount was far less than the $1.6M premium that was funded during his lifetime.

By the letter of contract law, Transamerica had the right to terminate coverage, but Mr. Lebbin and his family felt they had been misled. The policies were labeled "universal life"—surely they should cover him for his *whole life*. He had paid over $1.6 million in premiums during his life. The Lebbins sued Transamerica. As of publication of this book, the case remains in court. It garnered much attention, including an article in the *Wall Street Journal*.

If you are a trust officer, it's likely that you have a Mr. Lebbin in your portfolio of policies. Maturity provisions today are not as much of a concern for newer policies, as they are now designed to extend to age 120. Certain policies issued in the 1990s are a different story, however. Believe me, you do not want Mr. Lebbin's situation occurring on your watch. If you have such a situation, you want to discover it as soon as possible. This is why policy monitoring is so vital. If you catch a maturity provision early enough, you have options such as a policy exchange, surrender, or restructure. The longer one waits and the older the insured, the more limited are the options available.

I cannot stress enough how important it is for trustees and policyholders to seek out the maturity provisions in policies.

Here is some sample contractual language by policy type. This is by no means an exhaustive listing and has been taken from specific policies to make a point. It is not even a generalization as the majority of Whole Life policies have favorable maturity provisions. But, there are some that do not. My goal is to help trustees understand what to look for when requesting maturity provisions from carriers.

Examples of Maturity Provisions from Different Policy Types

Whole Life: "Benefit will mature or expire on the policy anniversary 2-17-2059" (Insured's age 98)

Universal Life: "This product is designed to mature on the anniversary date closest to the younger insured's age 98. The maturity date for this policy is August 21, 2023. If the policy matures by the passing of both insureds prior to the maturity date, then the policy proceeds will be the death benefit. Inversely, if the policy matures by age then policy proceeds will be the cash surrender value."

Variable Universal Life: "Final premium payment date is the policy anniversary nearest the younger insured's 95th birthday. No premiums may be paid after this date. The death proceeds after the final premium payment date will be the policy value less debt."

Since I originally published this book, it's become clearer to me that life settlements and maturity provisions are two vitally important elements of life insurance that trust officers must understand. A life settlement is a last resort—designed to help a policyholder get something out of a difficult situation. Meanwhile, maturity provisions can put a policyholder in an equally difficult situation. The job of a trust officer is to help their clients identify obstacles ahead and work to avoid them when possible. Our job at LifeTrust3D™ is to support trust officers, period. We do the background work and heavy lifting so trust officers can do what they do best: be proactive in addressing these difficult situations sooner, rather than waiting until it's too late. The more time we have to collaborate with the trust officer prior to future issues arising, more options are available to the client. It is when we are faced with short time horizons, such as policies lapsing in the near future or finding out about a maturity provision two or three years prior to its occurrence, that policy remediation alternatives are limited.

10

The *Best* Policy

"SO WHAT IS '*the best policy*,' anyway?" asked John, my newest client. A young and successful surgeon, John had been referred to me after an estate planning review with his attorney. He had been sold a policy a few years ago by another agent and had come into my office to get a fresh perspective, frustrated with his policy's performance in comparison to what originally had been promised.

The first thing out of his mouth had been, "Thanks for meeting with me. I'm concerned I was sold a bill of goods, and now I don't understand my policy. I thought it was the best policy for me, but now I'm not so sure. The agent who sold it to me was my father's friend, but he's now retired, and I don't know where else to turn."

"Well, John," I said, "I can't perform surgery, so it's unfair to ask *you* to understand all the ins and outs of life insurance. What I *am* able to do is help you better understand your current life insurance policy and evaluate your options. Then, once we agree on the appropriate path forward, our firm will assist you in monitoring and managing the plan so you don't get off course again. How does that sound?"

John looked at me blankly and said, "You mean you're not going to try to sell me something?"

With a big smile on my face, I said, "I wouldn't go that far now," and we laughed together.

"Think of it this way," I said. "Why did you purchase the policy initially? Is that reason still relevant?"

It turned out that John was disappointed in the policy's cash value accumulation. This was secondary, though, as his primary motivation for purchasing life insurance was to provide a substantial death benefit to his wife and two young children should he pass away before them.

John and I talked for almost an hour about his goals and hopes for his policy, and how they might have changed even over a short-term horizon. We were able to confirm that the policy he'd originally purchased was indeed the best one for him based on him completing our trademarked process, which included a benchmarking study of his policy compared to alternatives available in today's life insurance marketplace. Creating *the best policy* for John, as it turned out, meant the same thing it means for approximately 75 percent of the policies we review: either the policy is fine the way it is or a slight modification to the existing policy can get it back on track.

Life insurance is a curiously personalized beast. My role with John was simply to listen, assess the situation, and provide an objective framework for him to make an educated and informed decision. Based on the information we had already gathered before John came in, I had a notion that maintaining his current policy would provide the *best* outcome for John. However, it was important for him to be part of the process and understand it for himself. My goal was for him to have greater confidence in his life insurance policy . . . and maybe even love it again. Well, maybe he wouldn't love the policy itself, but I thought perhaps he would love and appreciate the protection and security it could provide for the ones he loved most in this world.

As I've said, there's no "one size fits all" with life insurance. We fully recognize that the purchase of a policy is only the beginning. Change is inevitable. Political and economic factors constantly affect policies and their purpose in a plan. Estate tax laws, insurance carrier strength, the health of the insured, the policy's performance, the grantor's ability to gift funds to the trust—these are all influencing factors that are in constant flux. Assess and reassess the goals and performance of your clients' life insurance portfolios in the face of an ever-changing world, and in doing so, you'll have taken the most crucial step in ensuring that the policy supports your client's needs and goals.

Each adjustment you make to policies to meet clients' needs within these changes must be deliberate and well documented. It's the same reason we monitor policies annually rather than simply accepting an annual policy *statement*: The devil is in the details, and when a choice that isn't backed by careful thought is put into play, those details can be overlooked and cause problems down the line. When people purchase these policies, they're not just purchasing a product or purchasing a policy for themselves. They're purchasing a promise that their policy will serve them and the ones they love most today and into the future. We want them to be able to see the fruits of that promise. During that meeting, John was sold something after all—not a product, but a *promise* that LifeTrust3D™, would commit to monitoring his life insurance policy annually on a fee basis. I smiled at him and said, "See, I told you I might sell you something."

John replied, much more seriously than I'd anticipated, "No, Tate, you didn't sell me. I knew our family needed your help, and my attorney told me you would take good care of us. I want to work with your firm, and will happily do so. Your fee reflects that value you will be providing to us."

We shook hands, and I prepared to see him out of the office. Before we got to the door, though, he stopped me.

"Wait," he said. "You never told me what '*the best policy*' is!"

I smiled. "Actually, John, I've been telling you all along. *The best policy* is the one that's right for *you*!"

After John left my office, I sat silently for a bit. I couldn't help but think of myself years before, as fresh-faced as John, and yet somehow listening to one of the wealthiest men in our community tell me about his hopes and fears: Charles. He'd trusted me, and together, we'd made decisions that had worked. He purchased a promise from me, and I was able to see it through. That promise has impacted every policy I've sold or managed since.

I thought of Henry Colton and the values he'd instilled in my father, who so graciously passed them to me and my brother. I thought of the $100,000 trust distributions that landed in Gary's three daughters' personal bank accounts that Christmas Eve a few years earlier. I thought of all my younger clients with young families they love and want to protect. I thought of Celeste and her family, and I thought of Michael and the thank you note he sent me.

That meeting with John was a culmination of many stories and experiences for me. When John and I shook hands at the end of our meeting, I thought back to a sermon I'd heard that hit me like a ton of bricks.

The Chinese bamboo needs careful attention and nourishment to establish a secure and intricate root system. Crafting this foundation requires a significant investment of time and energy, and a little love—but if you can dedicate yourself to that investment, your bamboo will flourish. You'll have a vibrant, living thing that can support itself as long as you provide it with what it needs: fertilizer, water, and protection from the weather.

The same is true of trust-owned life insurance. Only with the appropriate attention and nourishment can it flourish. Clients need a trust that they can indeed *trust*, and in order to get that, they need a team of advisors and a life insurance policy they can trust as well. The path to a trustworthy life insurance portfolio? Creating and nourishing that *best policy,* the one created specifically for the client, monitored consistently for the client, while always being mindful that it's not necessarily *for* the client—but for their loved ones.

Acknowledgments

My family in 2015, at Max Patch in Waynesville, NC, when I wrote the first edition of this book.

My family in 2019 at the Biltmore Estate in Asheville, NC. Look how much has changed since— my oldest son is now almost taller than me!

I AM WHERE I am today because of my faith, family, and friends.

First, I give thanks to God, who is good.

To Anna, my wife: You are the most amazing and beautiful woman I have ever known, and I still have to pinch myself to believe that I wasn't dreaming when you said yes. Thank you for always supporting me, loving me, and believing in me (even when I didn't). I cherish you and every second of our journey together.

To my wonderful children, Davis, Lillian, and Evan: You bring out the best in me, and I want to make you proud. You have taught me and your mom the true meaning of love. Lillian and Evan, you both have been incredible fighters in your lives and proven that you are survivors. You are my superheroes. Davis, being the oldest isn't always easy, but you represent all that is good in this world. You are an incredible young man. Davis, Lillian and Evan, you make being a father the greatest joy and blessing imaginable! God has blessed the three of you with incredible gifts; share them graciously and stay faithful.

Dad and Matt: Getting to work with my two best friends doesn't even seem fair. I would put the three of us up against anyone. Dad, thank you for teaching me the business and investing in me. I may not have a master's degree, but I have the only PhD from the George Groome School of Business (and Life) in the entire country! This book is dedicated to you. It is amazing what you have created and how many lives you have touched along the way. Thank you for all the seeds you have planted and nourished. Seeing them flourish together is a blessing. Matt and I are so fortunate to have a teacher, mentor, friend, and father in you. Matt, co-bro, I can't believe how far we've come together. You are the guy I want next to me in business and in life. You are my best friend and I don't tell you enough, but I love you.

Mom: Thanks for saying convincing Dad to say yes on that day in May 2003 when I called asking if I could come work with him. (Remember—he had to call me back that night so he could go home and ask your permission?) You are the glue that holds our family together, and the best person I know. Thank you for loving all of us as you do. You are truly an angel.

To the late Henry Colton: You taught my father so much that is now ingrained in me. You had the best sense of humor, but my favorite line of yours will always be, "Don't say 'Boo-Boo' when just 'Boo' will do."

To the Colton family: Thank you for taking my dad into your home. Not a day goes by that he doesn't pay homage to Henry and your family. When a new client comes in, we always open with: "Colton Groome Insurance Advisors, Inc. was founded on October 1, 1950, by Henry Colton. Henry was educated as an engineer at Yale, flew over twenty combat missions during World War II, survived, and came back to make the law review at the University of North Carolina at Chapel Hill. When you combine the precision of an engineer, the courage of a World War II combat aviator, and the thoroughness of an attorney, that is the fabric and foundation upon which our firm was built." I can't tell you how many times I leaned on Henry's legacy in our community when I first came into the industry as a young man. We will be forever grateful to the Coltons.

To the estate planning attorneys, national bank trust officers, and community bankers who have entrusted your most precious client relationships to me and our firm: Thank you. You are the reason we created LifeTrust3D™, and the reason I wrote this book. I am grateful to call you all my friends and colleagues.

To my clients: Without your trust and confidence, none of this would be possible. Some of you have known me since I was in diapers; some of you I grew up with; some of you I've met as an adult; and many of you are spread across the US and we've never met personally. However, your stories, families, and lives touch mine every day. I am forever thankful for all of you.

Finally, I have been fortunate to cross paths with three people and one organization that have had a tremendous impact in my professional career:

1. Larry J. Rybka: As the leader of Valmark Financial Group, you have freely shared your time and expertise with me as I made my way in this crazy business we call life insurance. Although you support hundreds of producers nationwide, I always feel like you have time for me and that you have a special interest in my success. You lead by doing things the right way with Christian principles and following the Golden Rule; it is easy to follow a leader like you.

2. Valmark Financial Group: You are more than a broker-dealer; you are like family. A special thanks to Tom Love for his contributions in chapter 4. Also, the diagrams, charts, and graphics are all from Valmark Financial Group. I thank you for sharing your expertise and always challenging your advisors to be our best. Moving our broker-dealer to Valmark was the single most impactful business decision Colton Groome Insurance Advisors ever made. Thank you for being exceptional.

3. Mike Pepe: From pizza to life insurance . . . to TOLI Vault, to Proformex. Who would have thought that happenstance meeting at the bar far away from both of our homes would have turned into this? I cannot believe what you have created in what is now Proformex. It is, hands down, the *best* ILIT administration platform in our business. I am so proud of what you have accomplished, and proud to call you my friend.

4. Robert Berman: Our fearless friend Robert Berman, who gave me the courage to write and publish the first edition of this book in 2014, left our world at the end of 2017 at the age of just fifty-three. Robert left three children that he loved dearly and a life partner, Stephanie, who made his world

go round. Robert's death teaches us all that life is fleeting, so love those close to you and plan for the unexpected. Good health and good fortune are not givens and can be taken at any time. Here are my original comments from 2014. They still hold true: "Yes, I saved you for last! Man, you gave me the confidence to pull all of this off. I can't believe how far we have come. Thanks for pushing me and believing in me. You are incredibly talented, and I admire your ability to just get things done. That is uncommon today in the business development world, but you make it seem simple. I am so grateful to have you on my team." I hope I've made you proud.

About the Author

G. Tate Groome is the founder and driving force behind LifeTrust3D™ and the motivation and heart behind *The Best Policy*. He is a Certified Financial Planner™ and Chartered Life Underwriter®, and most recently an Accredited Estate Planner®. He  has over fifteen years of experience in providing trusted life insurance solutions to individuals, trustees, and businesses. He recently won the distinguished "40 under 40" award in Asheville, NC, and is a recipient of the North Carolina Volunteer Award, chosen by the governor of the state. He earned two degrees from UNC Chapel Hill.

Prior to forming LifeTrust3D™, Tate taught elementary education and coached basketball for at-risk youth. He then began working for Colton Groome Insurance

Advisors, where he is also a principal, along with his brother and father. Tate serves on several boards: the YMCA of Western North Carolina, South Buncombe Youth Basketball, Asheville- Buncombe Technical College Foundation and Skyland United Methodist Church. He also coaches the basketball teams on which his three children play. Tate is happily married to the love of his life Anna. Tate and his family live in Asheville, NC.

Tate is available to speak at conferences, seminars, trade shows, association meetings, and corporate events. LifeTrust3D™ also offers certified continuing education classes (in person and online) for trustees, attorneys, and CPAs. ***To contact Tate and LifeTrust3D™ for seminars, speaking engagements, classes, and more****:*

G. Tate Groome, CFP®, CLU®, AEP®
Managing Partner, LifeTrust3D™
Toll-free: 844-747-5833
Fax: 828-254-5895
1127-B Hendersonville Road
Asheville, NC 28803
www.LifeTrust3D.com
www.tategroome.com